* SIMPLE *
SABOTAGE

✳ SIMPLE ✳ SABOTAGE

A MODERN FIELD MANUAL
FOR DETECTING AND ROOTING
OUT EVERYDAY BEHAVIORS THAT
UNDERMINE YOUR WORKPLACE

ROBERT M. GALFORD,
BOB FRISCH & CARY GREENE

HarperOne
An Imprint of HarperCollinsPublishers

HarperOne

HarperCollins books may be purchased for educational, business,
or sales promotional use. For information please e-mail the Special
Markets Department at SPsales@harpercollins.com.

HarperCollins website: http://www.harpercollins.com

HarperCollins®, 📖®, and HarperOne™ are trademarks of
HarperCollins Publishers.

FIRST EDITION

Designed by Ralph Fowler

Library of Congress Cataloging-in-Publication Data is
available upon request.

ISBN 978-0-06-237160-7

15 16 17 18 19   RRD(H)   10 9 8 7 6 5 4 3 2 1

To Susan, Katy, and Luke

Jacob, Adam, Noah, and Rachael

Jennifer, Ethan, and Eva

Contents

Introduction...1

Unintentional Sabotage May Be Destroying
Your Organization

1 Sabotage by Obedience...11

"Insist on Doing Everything Through Channels"

2 Sabotage by Speech...39

"Talk as Frequently as Possible and at Great Length"

3 Sabotage by Committee...63

"When Possible, Refer All Matters to Committees"

4 Sabotage by Irrelevant Issues...87

"Bring Up Irrelevant Issues as Frequently as Possible"

5 Sabotage by Haggling...107

"Haggle Over Precise Wordings of Communications"

6   Sabotage by Reopening Decisions...133

"Refer Back to Matters Decided Upon at the
Last Meeting"

7   Sabotage by Excessive Caution...155

"Urge Your Fellow-Conferees to Be 'Reasonable'
and Avoid Haste"

8   Sabotage by Is-It-Really-
Our-Call?...173

"Be Worried About the Propriety of Any Decision"

9   Modern Sabotage by CC: Everyone...193

"Send Updates as Frequently as Possible, Including
Anyone Even Peripherally Involved"

Acknowledgments...205
Notes...207
About the Authors...211

* SIMPLE *
SABOTAGE

Introduction

I n January 1944, at the height of World War II, the Office of Strategic Services (OSS)—the predecessor of today's Central Intelligence Agency—published an extraordinary classified document. OSS operatives, under the direction of General William J. "Wild Bill" Donovan, had been organizing and training members of the European resistance movement in tactics of sabotage. These techniques were presented in a slim volume, the *Simple Sabotage Field Manual,* which was printed in several languages and smuggled to Allied supporters behind enemy lines. The *Manual* detailed easy ways to disrupt and demoralize the enemy's institutions without being detected. The authors' intentions were clear: "Slashing tires, draining fuel tanks, starting fires, starting arguments, acting stupidly, short-circuiting electric systems, abrading machine parts will waste materials, manpower and time. Occurring on a wide scale, simple sabotage will be a constant and tangible drag on the war efforts of the enemy."

The cumulative effect of these thousands of barely detectable individual acts would wear down the Axis powers and prevent them from achieving their goals. While planes and tanks and ships battled the enemy on the front, the OSS and resistance fighters would use the techniques from the *Manual* to attack from within.

Much of the volume was devoted to physical acts of sabotage—of the put-sand-in-the-gas-tank or leave-oily-rags-in-a-pile variety. It advocated leaving "saws slightly twisted when you are not using them" as they would then eventually break when in use. It suggested clogging lubrication systems with any available substance. "Twisted combings of human hair, pieces of string, dead insects, and many other common objects," the book advised, "will be effective in stopping or hindering the flow of oil through feed lines and filters." It recommended sprinkling "rock salt or ordinary salt profusely over the electrical connections of switch points and on the ground nearby. When it rains, the switch will be short-circuited."

Cooling systems, fuel lines, railroad switches, electric motors, gears, telephones, toilets, tires—the

Manual had great advice on how to cause trouble all around, and how to not attract attention while doing so.

But one section of the *Manual* was devoted entirely to the methodical disruption of the enemy's *organizations*—in particular, their decision-making processes and the efficacy of their meetings and procedures.

The tactics described in this section were incredibly subtle—and devastatingly destructive. They were like viruses, piggybacking on normally benign activities as they spread and accumulated. And, like viruses, they carried the ability to weaken or render impotent the organizational infrastructure of the enemy. They were also difficult to spot, challenging to mitigate or reverse, and almost impossible to prevent.

These are the eight tactics from the *Simple Sabotage Field Manual*:

1. "Insist on doing everything through 'channels.' Never permit short-cuts to be taken in order to expedite decisions."

2. "Make 'speeches.' Talk as frequently as possible and at great length. Illustrate your 'points' by long anecdotes and accounts of personal experiences. Never hesitate to make a few appropriate 'patriotic' comments."

3. "When possible, refer all matters to committees, for 'further study and consideration.' Attempt to make the committees as large as possible—never less than five."

4. "Bring up irrelevant issues as frequently as possible."

5. "Haggle over precise wordings of communications, minutes, resolutions."

6. "Refer back to matters decided upon at the last meeting and attempt to re-open the question of the advisability of that decision."

7. "Advocate 'caution.' Be 'reasonable' and urge your fellow-conferees to be 'reasonable' and avoid haste which might result in embarrassments or difficulties later on."

8. "Be worried about the propriety of any decision—raise the question of whether such action as is contemplated lies within the jurisdiction of the group or whether it might conflict with the policy of some higher echelon."[1]

These eight tactics sound relatively harmless, don't they? In fact, aren't they aspects of the very behaviors that are necessary to the *health* of any group of people working together? For example, "channels"

DECLASSIFIED

tors to cause power leakage. It will be quite easy, too, for them to tie a piece of very heavy string several times back and forth between two parallel transmission lines, winding it several turns around the wire each time. Beforehand, the string should be heavily saturated with salt and then dried. When it rains, the string becomes a conductor, and a short-circuit will result.

(11) *General Interference with Organizations and Production*

(a) Organizations and Conferences

(1) Insist on doing everything through "channels." Never permit short-cuts to be taken in order to expedite decisions.

(2) Make "speeches." Talk as frequently as possible and at great length. Illustrate your "points" by long anecdotes and accounts of personal experiences. Never hesitate to make a few appropriate "patriotic" comments.

(3) When possible, refer all matters to committees, for "further study and consideration." Attempt to make the committees as large as possible — never less than five.

(4) Bring up irrelevant issues as frequently as possible.

(5) Haggle over precise wordings of communications, minutes, resolutions.

(6) Refer back to matters decided upon at the last meeting and attempt to re-open the question of the advisability of that decision.

(7) Advocate "caution." Be "reasonable" and urge your fellow-conferees to be "reasonable" and avoid haste which might result in embarrassments or difficulties later on.

(8) Be worried about the propriety of any decision — raise the question of whether such action as is contemplated lies within the jurisdiction of the group or whether it might conflict with the policy of some higher echelon.

DECLASSIFIED

The eight tactics for interfering with organizations and production from the *Simple Sabotage Field Manual*, 1944.

are important. They're vital communications tools that ensure that ideas are vetted thoroughly and that once a decision is made, the resources and skills needed to go forward with implementation are there. "Caution" is important too. If people threw caution to the winds and constantly took a Ready–Fire–Aim approach, chaos would reign.

Bear in mind: The OSS anticipated just that reaction. OSS leaders didn't want members of the Resistance caught and killed. That's why the tactics they taught had strong plausible deniability. These are good behaviors, but taken to an extreme. That's why they are insidious.

This was powerful stuff in 1944 and remains so today. Although the *Manual* has long been declassified, the acts of sabotage recommended in it are no less subtle and no less corrosive than they were more than seventy years ago. What's more, *they occur every day and all around the world in all sizes and types of working groups, from global corporations and nonprofits, to school and church committees, to small businesses.* Some of them, no doubt, occur in yours.

We are not suggesting that enemies are lurking in your midst. It's unlikely that you've got an internal resistance movement doggedly working to keep you from achieving your goals. But the odds are great that some individuals have unwittingly taken a page or two from the *Manual*. Left unchecked, their behaviors will, at the least, undermine your group or

organization, slowing down its—and *your*—best efforts. In the worst-case scenario, they will grind the
gears to a halt.

We've shared this list of OSS tactics with hundreds
of our friends, colleagues, and clients. Almost every
time they've responded with a chuckle, "That list de-
scribes my [department, company, volunteer group,
book club, board]—pick one; we've heard them all."

That's why we wrote this book. In our decades of
experience working with individuals and groups in
organizations large, small, public, private, and nonprofit, we've seen these corrosive tactics at work. We've
witnessed the damage they do, and we've worked with
clients across industries and continents to devise ways
to recognize, counteract, and prevent them.

The OSS presented eight tactics for sabotaging an
organization. This book tackles one in each chapter.
In the process of writing about the countermeasures
to these tactics, however, we've also realized that
as new organizational forms have taken shape and
new technologies have emerged over the past few decades, so have new opportunities to throw a monkey
wrench into the works. So we devote an additional
chapter to one of the most effective (which is to say
damaging) new tactics of sabotage that have become
commonplace since the *Manual* was written.

You will probably find most of the sabotage techniques discussed in this book familiar. You might
even laugh at some of them, thinking they are nothing

more than some people's quirky or annoying behaviors. You might believe that they are easily corrected. "Well," you might think, "I can just point these things out to my colleagues, or direct reports, or even my boss, and the behaviors will stop; problem solved."

But rooting out these corrosive behaviors isn't so simple, since they are often mutant excesses of laudable aspects of organizational life and group behavior—enforcing rules, checking that processes have been followed correctly, involving co-workers in decisions and seeing that decisions are made in the right way. Slowly, these behaviors become part of the working culture, and spotting them, much less extricating them, isn't easy. Exposing and inoculating any working group against sabotage requires several stages:

Identify: Spot sabotage as it occurs, and help others see when a positive behavior has crossed the line into becoming counterproductive or destructive.

Calibrate: Put into place the right expectation for tolerance—the range of acceptable behaviors—so that productive behavior is encouraged, but sabotage is prevented.

Remediate: Give everyone in the organization the permission, the language, and the techniques to call out damaging behaviors in a constructive way.

Inoculate: Introduce tools, metrics, and process changes to prevent the sabotage from recurring (or from occurring in the first place) and to help develop a low-sabotage culture.

In practice, these stages are sometimes sequential (as we've written them here), but more often, they have to happen at the same time (as we often treat them in the chapters to come). It depends on the type of sabotage, who spots it (and what sort of control that person has over the group), why the sabotage is occurring, and what type of group you're dealing with.

As lifelong strategists, the three of us have read many books promising dramatic breakthroughs or offering radical ways to rethink how organizations are run. This book isn't one of those. *Simple Sabotage* is about the day-to-day routine interactions and processes we rely on as we work that are undermined by unintentional sabotage. By identifying and removing the hundreds or even thousands of small, barely perceptible irritants—the "sand" that clogs the machinery—you will transform your workplace or workgroup experience and the experience of those around you. You will increase your effectiveness, spur creativity, and improve working relationships. Whether you're in the middle of the sabotage or you're managing a department, division, or company where sabotage is under way; whether you're a committee member, a front-line worker, or a C-Suite executive—we'll show you how to help your group become as productive as it can be.

1

Sabotage by Obedience

Insist on doing everything
through channels. Never permit
shortcuts to be taken in order
to expedite decisions.

The deal was dead in the water. The company was going to lose a long-standing account. Michael knew it, but he couldn't do anything about it.

The client's representative, Samantha, had called unexpectedly, late in the afternoon, saying that a competing software firm had pitched a package deal—software, training, support—at a slightly lower rate than she was paying. The competitor was offering to include more training time. Although Michael's firm had already made its best-and-final offer, couldn't they sweeten it just a bit to match the competing bid? Samantha had to have an immediate answer; she needed to select the winning bid by the end of the day.

"I can't do that," Michael thought, feeling a weight in the pit of his stomach. At their most recent sales conference Michael's boss, the vice president of sales, had made it clear that all revisions to bid prices had to get either his or the division head's approval "in order to rein in some cowboy pricing that's been giving away the store."

Left to his own devices, Michael would have matched the competitor's offer. He knew Samantha's company well, and he felt sure that he could make up the difference with add-on services in just a few months. But he didn't have the authority to lower the bid, and he knew his boss, en route to Europe with the division head, was unreachable.

Michael isn't trying to sink his company. He's a hard worker. He loves his job. And he's just following the rules, which were created to ensure that the company's salespeople didn't jeopardize the company by promising things they couldn't profitably deliver. By insisting on going through channels—that is, adhering closely to the procedures put in place by his boss and division head and going to his bosses for approval for any and every situation that falls beyond the perceived scope of his position—Michael is technically doing the "right" thing.

But his good behavior is about to cost his company a contract. Michael knows that without those few minor—but unobtainable—concessions, the deal is finished. And losing this deal is, he knows, the wrong thing.

You'd think that saboteurs *wouldn't* be model employees or colleagues. You'd think that they would be the people who make a habit of trying to get around the rules, or taking lots of shortcuts. But Michael is what we call an "Obedient Saboteur." He doesn't stray from the guidelines set out in the employee handbook or in the processes and rules laid out by the head of the sales department. And it's his *adhering* to these rules, not *breaking* them, that's about to cost his company a customer.

Obedience—doing exactly what you're told to do, and not doing things outside your scope of authority—is usually a valuable behavior. It's predictable, and usually it means that you can work with confidence knowing you're not making mistakes. What's more, since you're "playing by the book," decision-making can often be reduced to "paint by numbers" simplicity. Organizations run more smoothly most of the time if everyone is following instructions set with no variability. But obedience becomes Sabotage by

Obedience—instantly—*when it prevents personal judgment from overriding processes that for whatever reason are not working at that moment.* That's what the OSS was counting on. That's what happened with Michael. And that's what might be happening in your organization.

When Does Obedience Look like Sabotage?

To tell when this type of sabotage is happening in your organization or group, start by examining the rules you have for governing behavior—formal or implied—and see whether you can explain why each one is there. Think about the kind of work you're trying to get done, the type of people you're working with, the nature of their roles, and the relative importance of their individual judgment on the broad objectives you're trying to accomplish.

For example, the leaders of a retail chain might consider whether their return department is there to help customers make returns rapidly and easily, with a minimum of fuss, or whether it is there to make sure returns are given only if they are justified and all the documentation is in place. Clearly, there's a balance point between the two. But which is more important? Is that balance point right in the middle?

Or is customer convenience more or less important than preventing possible fraud losses?

Then ask: If people had complete freedom to make decisions on their own, at what point would that freedom begin to get you in trouble? Medicine comes to mind as an industry where adherence to procedures and protocols is paramount. And we're not sure we would be thrilled about food safety inspectors deciding on their own what criteria to use before approving a batch of ingredients.

On the other hand, how much freedom from process do people need in order to be creative, innovative, responsive, and effective in the moment? Suppose a candidate for a minister position contacts the hiring committee to ask some background questions before the interview, and the committee chair is away on vacation? Can someone else answer the candidate's questions to ensure that the candidate doesn't lose interest in the position?

What overall message does your group's culture send about doing things by the book and through channels? And *why* is that particular message being sent? Is it by design, that is, consciously controlled? Or is it the inadvertent result of hundreds of decisions and policies that have accumulated over time? Should this message still apply? Should it apply across the board to all group members?

The answers to these questions will give you a pretty good understanding of what procedures or norms of behavior are a must—that is, when it is absolutely imperative to go through channels—and when more freedom ought to be allowed. Armed with that knowledge, you can then begin to figure out who might be doing some serious damage by being too good at following the rules.

Senior leaders at Shepley Bulfinch, a prominent national architectural firm, ask these questions of themselves regularly as they strive to refine the firm's processes for evaluating its pipeline of work. Like many professional services firms, the company asks its principals and project managers to submit regular reports on their upcoming workload. But at one time, managers were required to include in those reports *all* projects in their pipelines—and the company found itself "blessed," temporarily, with a number of Obedient Saboteurs who were happy to comply. These managers did just as they were told, including every project in the reports even if it seemed that unpredictable variables might delay some jobs. Other, more realistic, staff did not follow the rules completely. They held back, either excluding risky projects from their reports or at least painting a more conservative picture of timing.

Simply letting the saboteurs go through channels and follow the prescribed submission procedure was creating inaccurate reports that increased the risk of haphazard resource allocation and recurring feast-or-famine situations. So Shepley Bulfinch leaders had to figure out whether it was more important to have an incorrect report than no report at all—or whether they needed to create a third option.

They went with the third option. Project leaders now meet more regularly with the firm's CFO to create a balanced forecasting mechanism, and managers are routinely encouraged to annotate their forecasts. Identifying when obedience was leading to unwitting sabotage was the first step toward correcting the problem.

Michael Glazer, CEO of the $1.6 billion NYSE retailer Stage Stores, is also constantly assessing company rules. In fact, he told us that when he became CEO, one of the first things he did was to try to get a handle on *why* certain rules were in place so he could evaluate them effectively. The previous management team had been focused almost entirely on margins. As a result, they had enacted rules regarding purchasing to ensure that margins wouldn't be too thin. Maybe those rules had saved the company from financial ruin at some point—Glazer didn't know. What he did know was that when he came on board, Stage Stores buyers were not allowed to stock some of the most attractive, in-demand lines of clothing.

"We had only a very small selection of Nike," he said. "Our customers would go to our stores looking for brands like Nike and leave unhappy and empty-handed. We forced them to do business with our competitors. Yes, we could make only a thin margin with some popular brands. But if a customer walked out with two tops and a jacket in addition to the Nikes they came in for, we would have made a nice total margin on that overall purchase. The buyers were following a directive that had come right from our senior management team, but their obedience was hurting the business. And they knew it; they just couldn't do anything about it."

Glazer, too, is concerned with margins. But once he realized how the existing rules were actually doing harm to the business overall, he started to reevaluate and rework them so that they now guide the company's buyers but are not so rigid that they prevent buyers from making purchasing decisions that will ultimately help the bottom line.

The Bell Curve Test

You probably know who the squeaky wheels are in your group. These are the people who are out of line a lot; they probably try your nerves. But they're easy to spot. To ferret out the Obedient Saboteurs (and the flawed rules they may be following), you have to look for the people who don't make any noise at all.

Suppose, for example, you have a night manager of a hotel authorized to provide room upgrades to late-arriving guests. That person can give an upgrade to everyone who walks through the door, or he or

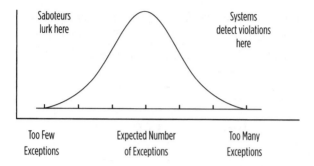

Saboteurs lurk here

Systems detect violations here

Too Few Exceptions

Expected Number of Exceptions

Too Many Exceptions

she may never give an upgrade at all. You can probably track this behavior pretty easily. To get a sense of where the norms are, create a bell curve where the middle of the curve shows the number of exceptions to the rule that you would expect to see. As the graphic shows, it will be clear, by looking at the far right side of the curve, which employees are pushing the limits on your guidelines—who is likely providing too many upgrades, or upgrades where none is warranted.

But it will also be clear who works at the other extreme—those managers who rarely, if ever, offer an upgrade. Ultimately, those people probably represent the more grievous threat. They're not your squeaky wheels. They're invisible. But their behavior is slowly, surely, building rigidity into your company—rigidity that can cause it to crack.

Not every organization regularly gathers the kind of data that make the bell curve test an easy exercise.

But if the data are there, particularly for customer-facing activities, then do the test. Exposing the "hidden" side of the curve is a big step toward eliminating Sabotage by Obedience.

Rehabilitate and Prevent Obedient Saboteurs

Once you spot individual Obedient Saboteurs, the remedy can take several forms. It might involve rewriting some of the rules that govern their work (like Shepley Bulfinch and Stage Stores did). But the solution might be much simpler (although not necessarily as easy as it sounds): reviewing the saboteur's job description or role and making it clear that that person's judgment is wanted and needed.

For example, if you're a supervisor and you suspect a lower-level employee of being an Obedient Saboteur, give that person some responsibility that occasionally requires him or her to make a personal judgment. Then follow through with coaching to make sure that he or she understands that a little risky behavior is okay even if the results don't always pan out.

If the person works at a high level, the antidote is more complex. A higher-level executive might be creating a culture within a department or function that discourages sensible rule-breaking, encourages "cover your rear" behavior, or both, across an entire team. In such cases, all of the team members need to understand their behavior's negative effects on the organization; the entire team may need some coaching.

To inoculate your organization or working group at a broader level against Obedient Saboteurs, and to make Sabotage by Obedience something that people can talk about comfortably, spot easily, and resolve as needed, take as many of the following four steps as apply to your situation.

Revisit Your Performance Metrics and Incentives

You want your metrics—the things you measure and the ways you measure them—to reinforce your processes *and* drive the outcomes you seek. You will inadvertently create Obedient Saboteurs if you reward people for adhering to the rules even when common sense tells them not to. To make sure that your metrics are not leading to sabotage, follow these steps:

> **Catalog the performance metrics you or your company track for each type of job under your supervision.** For example, a hotel chain might track how many complimentary room upgrades a front desk supervisor gives out.

Consider whether each metric is necessary. Does it affect the hotel if front desk supervisors give out too many or too few upgrades? It does. Hoteliers believe that giving away too many upgrades devalues the regular rooms and creates expectations that guests should get more than they're willing to pay for. Too few, however, is a lost opportunity to reward the best customers for their loyalty.

Identify the explicit link between each metric and higher profit. For a hotel, too many upgrades means higher cleaning costs, higher food costs, and lower guest satisfaction when guests are placed in a standard room.

Determine what behavior the obedient employee is expected to follow. The obedient front desk manager should provide the occasional upgrade to frequent guests but must be aware that each upgrade costs the company money.

Ask yourself, "What would happen if someone were to try to drive this metric to an extreme? Would that behavior still be desirable or lead to adverse outcomes?" In our example, the Obedient Saboteur would give out very few, if any, upgrades. In this case, frequent guests

who did deserve recognition for their loyalty
would not receive any and potentially take
their business elsewhere.

Set up your metrics to reveal extreme behaviors.
In this example, the measurement system is
designed to detect too many upgrades, not
too few. The Obedient Saboteur would likely
be undetected. The hotel should start flagging
front desk supervisors who give too few
upgrades relative to their peers, not the ones
giving out too many.

Sometimes your metrics will need to be qualita-
tive rather than quantitative. You may find that coming up with answers to the questions raised in each
step depends more on observation and judgment
than on hard numbers. In either case, by assessing
the right things, you'll create a net that's more likely
to catch a saboteur.

You might also want to keep an eye on your incentive programs. Sometimes, the incentives set up
for a temporary initiative will encourage employees
to "work the system" to their advantage and hurt the
company in the process. These employees probably
aren't even thinking about whether their behavior
is hurting the company. Their focus is on the task
and the reward. And since they are *obedient*—after

all, they are simply following the rules you've set for them—they're hard to spot.

A client of ours who was trying to get more retailers to carry one of its flagship products, bleach, launched a seasonal sales incentive program to encourage salespeople to open new accounts: For every new account that a salesperson opened, he or she would get an immediate cash bonus. The deal for new retail accounts was just as sweet: Unsold product could be returned for up to ninety days—and the account canceled—with no penalty.

Two weeks into the program, the company's CEO was driving by a gas station and noticed cases of his product stacked against the back of the building, in full sun (bleach needs to be stored away from heat, and of course a gas station isn't the usual place a consumer would go to buy bleach). It turned out that a salesperson had gone to his friend, the gas station owner, and told him to open an account and then return any unsold product after a few weeks.

Did the salesperson want to hurt the company— the source of his livelihood? No. The company's overall health wasn't on his radar. He wasn't thinking like a top manager. He was just following the carrot the company was dangling in front of him—putting "points on the scoreboard" squarely within the rules that had been created. The CEO, for his part, was blindsided. And you probably could have predicted that outcome.

Guard Against Extreme
"Continuous Improvement"

There's an old expression about dogs chasing cars. What will they do if they ever catch one? Similarly, some organizations chase a particular outcome or performance metric simply because they have become accustomed to the chase itself and have lost any sense of what a reasonable stopping point might be.

This problem can be particularly acute in organizations with a culture of "continuous improvement." Continuous improvement is a business philosophy created by W. Edwards Deming in the mid-twentieth century. This philosophy thinks of processes as systems and holds that if each component of the system constantly tries to both increase quality and reduce costs, efficiency and success will follow. But taken to an extreme, even continuous improvement can lead to sabotage.

One company we know had a call center manager driving his team to move from an average pickup speed of 1.4 rings to 1.2 rings. The division head asked, "How often do callers abandon us after only 1.4 rings?" "Almost never," he was told. "Virtually no callers who actually intended to call us hang up before the third ring." Yet the call center manager persisted in trying to ensure that all calls were answered more quickly each year. Why?

Because getting the phones answered quickly was

his job—by definition, quicker was better. He never thought to question whether he had crossed the threshold where process had overridden outcome. He had become one of the Obedient Saboteurs. If you asked him why he was trying to lower pickup times, he would tell you that faster pickup means improved customer experience. That's true—but the threshold is three rings. Once you get below three rings, faster pickup times don't continue to improve the customer's experience anymore. The problem we see, time after time, is that nobody bothers to go back and tell the call center managers of the world to go continuously improve something else.

To keep this kind of sabotage out of your group, step back and conduct a formal review of any continuous improvement programs you have in place. If they aren't relevant anymore, pull the plug.

But if these programs are still useful, figure out the point where they become too much of a good thing. If you don't know the answer ("two rings is good enough"), then it's time for some new analysis.

Finally, watch out for "improvement fatigue." Organizations, like people, can become addicted to self-improvement. We all have friends who, at one time or another, went to an extreme following the rules of a diet or exercise program beyond what was sensible. We know of one restaurant where employees were expected to reread the employee manual *on their breaks*. That's overkill. Don't exhaust people.

When people are worn down, they often follow the rules with glazed eyes and shut minds. They may not realize when a rule is hurting their ability to get work done well. And if you are one of the exhausted, speak up! In fact, consider calling (or asking for) a "continuous improvement holiday." Let employees off the treadmill for a week—and then ask them to reflect on the experience and offer their thoughts on the program, given some distance. After the break, they will be more likely to have an objective, balanced perspective on both the rules that help them and the rules that sometimes go too far.

Tolerate Mistakes and Celebrate Good Judgment

Sometimes when people use their own judgment, they're going to be wrong (read: they're going to make what you think is a bad decision). In the interests of the greater good, those mistakes must be tolerated. An old saying sums this up pretty well: "Good judgment comes from experience, and experience comes from bad judgment."

At one New England fire department, for example, all employees are allowed to talk to the press. Under the previous administration, only the chief talked to the press. When he wasn't available, the news outlets got a "no comment," which can seem awkward or evasive. What's more, too many "no comments" makes for frustrated reporters, which can be a bad thing when it's time for them to cover controversial topics, such as increased budgets. The new chief knows that the firefighters, medics, and staff may not always say exactly what he would say and may stumble a few times. But he realizes that having some freedom in this area is important for personal development. He also knows that in an environment that has many very important protocols that need to be followed, it is important to remind people that their judgment is also important, so he is tolerant.

The chief has also made sure to prepare the department's members for the kinds of questions reporters may ask. He has set guidelines and explicit expectations: Be clear, be brief, stick to the facts, respect privacy laws.

To encourage tolerance in your own working group, try (or suggest trying) something we call the "Favorite Mistake Exercise." Here's how it works: Have everyone around the table tell a brief anecdote about a real mistake they have made, a didn't-end-well mistake that is probably difficult for them to talk about. In other words, this can't be one of those mistakes where they were late getting to a client's office, but when they arrived, they spotted smoke, saved the day by sounding the alarm, and the grateful client tripled the order. It has to be painful, and a lesson has to be learned the hard way as part of the outcome.

Most mistakes, stacked up against the ones that these exercises reveal, won't look so bad. And knowing that mistakes are relative, your employees may be more willing to stick their necks out for something they believe might do the company good.

But perhaps there's no better way to protect your organization against obedient sabotage than to *celebrate examples of when people use good judgment—* even if the person you're praising has broken the rules.

There's a story about a retired Federal Express pilot Captain Bernard Bourgeois that's apparently still well known among FedEx employees. As told by James Zeigenfuss, in his book, *Customer Friendly,* FedEx was just starting up, and Captain Bourgeois's plane was stuck on an airport ramp in Cleveland. The fledgling company was having trouble paying its bills, so Bourgeois couldn't get the two hundred gallons of fuel he needed to get back to FedEx's hub in Memphis.

Bourgeois called flight operations, and the person there asked him if he had a credit card. Bourgeois did, and used it to pay for the fuel so the company could stay on schedule. Reflecting on that night, Bourgeois later said, "I didn't know if I'd get my money back, but I figured, 'Well, what the hell.'"[1]

Buying that fuel violated the company's protocol. But the company celebrated his decision. By publicizing that event, and others in the same spirit, FedEx has built a culture of entrepreneurism and risk-taking.

Try (or suggest) running a very simple internal appreciation exercise. Set up an old-fashioned box in each department, or a dedicated email account, and encourage people to submit notes describing examples of intelligent rule-breaking or risk-taking that they've seen their colleagues do on the job. Screen them privately, of course, but read a few of these out loud at each meeting. You may be surprised at the things people notice; the subjects of the notes may also be surprised—and grateful for the small vote of appreciation.

Question and Test the Logic of Established Processes

If your group or organization does a lot of things simply because "That's the way we've always done them," it's probably time to give your processes a spring cleaning. You might find that you and your colleagues have been protecting processes that are doing more harm than good.

Consider: For many years, health insurance companies have insisted that patients get referrals from their primary care physicians before seeing a specialist. Do you know how often one major insurer checked to make sure that these referrals were justified? Less than 1 percent of the time. Yet patients and doctors spent hours seeking and giving referrals. Then that insurer decided to simply end the practice for some plans. It opened up the specialist network to patients so that they no longer needed to get a primary care referral. If patients needed to see a dermatologist, they simply went to see one.

A fraction of the resources formerly used to administer the referral bureaucracy was redeployed to track down the small percentage of people who appeared to overuse specialists, and guidelines were imposed for those individuals to access the specialist network. But for most patients in most cases, the new and more straightforward process was a welcome change. Ultimately, that plan increased customer satisfaction and significantly lowered its costs.

Here's a painless way to overhaul some of your processes. Put someone with experience through the new-employee orientation for that person's function. See whether he or she thinks new employees are being told to do the right things, for the right reasons.

If you are a manager at a larger organization, you might also consider conducting the occasional brief anonymous survey. Employees tell each other all the time what doesn't make sense about their jobs. But if you ask them directly, you may not get a candid answer. Every once in a while, ask them to confide their thoughts anonymously. But don't stick to the typical employee survey script.

A lot of employee surveys focus on "climate." The questions center on whether employees are getting good feedback from their bosses, or whether they are thinking of changing jobs, and why. Those aren't bad questions, but they won't show you whether your company is developing Obedient Saboteurs. Throw in some blunt questions about the company itself, such as:

- What is the stupidest rule or process we have around here?

- What are the three biggest obstacles you face in doing your job?

- If you could rewrite or change one process or procedure, what would it be and why?

Take the first question. Maybe the logic behind a so-called stupid rule has not been communicated the right way. Maybe people just don't understand why it's in place. If that's the case, then you can explain it.

On the flip side, maybe you'll find that a so-called stupid rule really *is* stupid. Maybe it made sense five or ten years ago when it was put in place, but it doesn't make sense now. If that's the case, you probably have some Obedient Saboteurs in your midst who are spending time (and money) enforcing the rule. If so, these rules are taking away from other work that could actually create value.

One manager we know was relentless about the procurement budget. The stupid rule he followed faithfully was that he wasn't allowed to bring any proposals for a component to his boss for review if the component was quoted at more than $4 per unit. The problem was that he was turning away potential suppliers—who might have negotiated great deals for the company with hefty ancillary benefits—if they submitted proposals for price points of, say, $4.05, or even $4.02 per unit. Blind devotion to the rules was winning out over sound business judgment—until this manager's boss found out at a chance meeting with a rejected supplier.

Most big companies—and even many small working groups and long-standing committees—don't turn like speedboats. They turn more like the *Queen Mary*. Besides being big, over time the ship becomes more difficult for the captain to turn: The connection between the wheelhouse and the rudder gets calcified; barnacles grow. When that happens, people have to walk around with a sledgehammer and get rid of the corrosion and barnacles. Your managers or group leaders—all of them—have to be willing to ask: "What part of doing things through channels do we *have* to do for the safety of employees and customers, and what part can we skip?" They have to be able to say: "It's great that you can predict the margins three years out to a decimal point. But I don't care. Doing that isn't really adding value. It's adding clutter. It's replacing content with process. Let's just end it, now.

Look at the meaning, the context of your decisions. Not just what the rules say we should be doing."

Small Irritants, Big Implications

It may seem like Obedient Saboteurs are more likely to lurk in stodgy old groups or big organizations with gnarly long roots of bureaucracy. But don't think you're immune from this kind of sabotage if you work at a small business or in a young, hip company with an open-concept floor plan and napping pods. As soon as your group starts to grow, or as soon as you're doing something for the second time and trying to avoid the mistakes you made the first time, your group is vulnerable. Watch out when you hear something like: "Last year, we got confused and overbought. So let's make it a rule that we have only one person buying supplies." That's your smoking gun.

The fact that Obedient Saboteurs are omnipresent and dangerous in all kinds of working groups and organizations—big and small—was recently illustrated by an experience a friend of ours had.

She went to buy a cup of coffee at a small convenience store and saw a sign that read, "Buy any size coffee, and pastries are 99 cents." She poured a cup, picked up a pastry, and went to the counter. The cashier rang it up and she paid, took her change, and turned to leave.

After a few steps she realized that she hadn't gotten the right change. The cashier had charged her 99 cents for the coffee and full price for the pastry. So she went back to the counter, and said, "Excuse me, but I think you gave me the wrong change. The coffee should have been full price, and the pastry should have been 99 cents."

The cashier looked at the change she was holding out and said, "No, the coffee is 99 cents." Our friend replied: "No, it's not. Look at the sign." The cashier studied the sign. It was undeniable: any size coffee, pastry 99 cents. She noticed that people were now forming a short line behind her. Then he said, "The pastry you bought isn't part of that deal."

Our friend pointed out that both the pastry and the coffee she had in her hand were exactly the same as those displayed on the sign offering the special price. The only thing that was different was the price the cashier was charging her.

The cashier was clearly getting frustrated, as a line of impatient people was growing behind our friend, and the people in it were fidgeting. Realizing she was at an impasse with the cashier, she scooped up her change, thanked him for his time and walked away. But then she took a moment to think about what had just occurred. The cashier didn't seem like an argumentative person. He was clearly not trying to cheat her. So she went back to the counter after there was no line.

"Let me ask you a question," she said. "You're not allowed to give refunds, even for just 39 cents, right?" "No," the cashier replied. "I need to get my manager's permission to give a refund, and he stepped out. He'll be back in a few minutes if you want to talk to him. Sorry, those are the rules."

Mystery solved. Case closed. The cashier was just following "the rules," and he had simply been stalling our friend until either the manager returned or she dropped the issue and walked away.

Nobody expects a corner convenience store to have customer service at the level of, say, Nordstrom. Obviously, cashiers can't be opening cash drawers and handing out refunds for whatever reasons they see fit. But in this case the pendulum had swung too far. By not allowing a cashier to use common sense to correct an error, no matter how minor, management had created an Obedient Saboteur who adhered to "the rules" and cost goodwill in the process.

It may seem like the issues that stem from employees or members of a group who are only too eager to follow procedures to a fault—the Obedient Saboteurs—are simply irritants. And you might think that putting up with these irritants is easier than dealing with them or preventing them in the first place. At the end of the day, can a person who always "plays by rules" really damage an organization? The answer is, yes.

Obedient Saboteurs are not harmless. Like the cashier whose inability to go around channels slowed down the line of paying customers and cost the convenience store one (our friend isn't going back to that store for a cup of coffee any time soon!), or like the hotel front desk manager who ticks off frequent travelers by constantly denying them room upgrades, Obedient Saboteurs can destroy the productivity of your group and rob it of its true potential. Detecting these insidious acts of sabotage might be tricky—but it's well worth the effort.

Imagine a checkpoint guard in a black-and-white World War II movie: The guard demands "Your papers, please," of a truck driver; he carefully scrutinizes both the documents and the driver before requiring a thorough search of a vehicle that he knows is likely to be perfectly harmless; he chuckles to himself as the line of trucks waiting to pass grows longer and longer. He is the very picture of the ruthless, careful agent of the state protecting the Fatherland and doing his part to undermine the war effort.

The equivalent is likely happening in your organization today, with the same corrosive effect.

2

Sabotage by Speech

Make "speeches." Talk as frequently
as possible and at great length.
Illustrate your "points" by
long anecdotes and accounts
of personal experiences.

People who talk too much are annoying, but
can they really be saboteurs? Absolutely.
"Speeches" don't have to be long to do damage. They just have to be long *enough*. And they don't
have to be given from a podium.

Picture the World War II OSS-directed saboteur,
working undercover in enemy territory in the management ranks for the railroad. He attends a meeting
at which decisions are supposed to be made about
the coming week's schedule, moving military supplies, and coordinating with passenger train service.

During the meeting, he stops the action several times by offering a piece of useful advice and then saying "in other words," and offering the same advice again, with different language, and maybe an example or two from his prewar experience as a transportation expert in the private sector. He's interesting to listen to; no one minds that he tends to be a "Long Talker." In fact, people welcome his stories. However, the group has only one hour allotted for the meeting; by the end, several decisions still remain to be made. The leader quickly delegates the other decisions without fully discussing them.

Nothing seems amiss. But later that week, a passenger train is blocking a station where a military train is supposed to be unloading supplies, causing a domino-effect delay in getting the supplies to their final destination. No one thinks to blame the Long Talker. The heat falls on the people who were left to make the decisions after the meeting broke up.

When OSS staff members came up with this tactic of "make speeches," they didn't mean the kind where someone books a room and a podium. They meant going on and on at every possible opportunity— especially during meetings. There's nothing specifically wrong about occasionally indulging in monologues at staff meetings. When done right, they can inspire, inform, and direct. They can call people to action.

But talking too much, too frequently, can delay or derail a discussion long enough to make everyone just a little late for their next task and maybe just confused enough, agitated enough—or dulled enough—to make a mistake. That's what the OSS was counting on. And that's why it's important to take seriously the various kinds of speech sabotage that happen in working groups.

The first step to countering Sabotage by Speech is to understand the many forms it can take. In this chapter we'll go over six types of Speech Saboteurs that you may find familiar. Mostly, as we've said, they lurk in meetings. But sometimes, they can spring out at you in the corridors, or even in the restroom. Later, we'll provide our top tactics for stopping their damaging behavior from undermining your—and your group's—goals.

Meet the Speech Saboteurs

Clearly, we all need to talk; we need to contribute to conversations and participate in meetings in order to get our work done. And clearly, some people are better communicators than others. What's more, all of us have the occasional "off day" when we talk more than we should, fail to articulate a point and meander in our explanations, or take a conversation off topic. Some people, though, are chronic offenders and repeatedly engage in Sabotage by Speech that derails our meetings and conversations and wastes our time. We've all seen the six types of Speech Saboteurs at work, however innocently, in situations personal and professional and in groups large and small.

The Long Talker

The online Urban Dictionary defines a Long Talker as "a person who can't shut up, usually spewing on about themselves and/or their day. They typically don't know when they are 'Long Talking' and/or how much the other person and/or people who are listening to them want him/her to shut up."[1]

Long Talkers go on and on every time they speak—whether on a conference call or a video chat or at a meeting in person. When they are asked a question, they never answer with a quick "yes" or "no." Instead, they say, "Yes and let me tell you why . . ." or "No and you know what? This reminds me of the time when . . ." They are always too eager to share that anecdote from their past that relates in some remote way to the topic of the meeting.

This behavior is valuable much of the time. Maybe a Long Talker is older and more experienced than others in the meeting, and many of his or her

stories help the others develop their ability to ana-
lyze problems or learn how to be objective in charged
situations.

So when is it sabotage? When other people at
the meeting already understand the point the Long
Talker is going to make and don't need a long story
to illustrate it. When the other people already agree
with the Long Talker. When other items on the
agenda need attention and time is tight. When the
meeting is over and people need to get out already
and get on with their work. That is, when the benefits of the long stories are likely to be outweighed by
the negative consequences that result from the time
spent listening to them. Long Talkers rob us of our
time.

The Tangent Talker

Tangent Talkers barrel off in a direction that may
only marginally relate to what the meeting is about,
if it relates at all. Sometimes they do this because
they haven't followed the conversation—they're day-
dreaming or checking email—and sometimes they
haven't understood the conversation. Say the group
has been talking about a decision to buy new software; the Tangent Talker pipes up with a comment—
and maybe a question—about buying new hardware.

When should this behavior be tolerated? When
the person clearly articulates a good reason for

bringing up the new topic, and the expectations for what's going to happen are reasonable; that is, when there is no expectation that any major decision-making will be made on the fly. If, for example, the conversation is about whether to install new software that will help eliminate redundancies in the finance department, but the Tangent Talker points out that the hardware in which the software will be installed is almost obsolete, then you've got a valid tangent on the table.

This behavior should also be tolerated when Tangent Talkers are important to the group for reasons other than their input. For example, if the Tangent Talker's endorsement is important for organizational or political purposes—when this person has a lot of sway—then you're stuck listening to him or her, but for a good reason.

Additionally, this behavior can be tolerated without too much worry in situations where it has taken a lot of effort to get a particular group of people together. Maybe one individual is based in Hong Kong, two in London, and one in Boston. Maybe their schedules or time zones rarely permit face-to-face meetings. The value these people can generate when they're in a room together, as opposed to on a video-conference or phone call, can sometimes outweigh the cost of a tangent or two.

But other than these exceptions, this behavior is sabotage.

Here's an example, told to us by a patient integrator at one of the largest medical centers in the
United States. He and his co-workers are frontline
employees—that is, they are the first people with
whom a patient or caregiver comes in contact when
referred to the center for treatment.

His boss called a meeting to bring the frontline
people together with managers in various cancer-
care departments at one of their principal hospitals.
The goal? To help everyone understand one another's roles so that they could work together more
seamlessly.

For forty-five minutes the conversation stayed
on target, as everyone introduced themselves and
engaged in an exercise that led to a meaningful discussion about what everyone present could do to
improve the connections among the various departments. Goal accomplished. Right? Not so fast.

At the end of the meeting, the moderator opened
up the floor for further discussion by asking, "If
there's anything more to say, we do have a little bit
more time." And that's when a department manager,
emboldened by the invitation and the fact that fifteen minutes were left in the meeting, started talking
about processes in his department and his management techniques that were not directly related to the
topic of the meeting. This, of course, encouraged
other managers, not to be outdone, to chime in with
their processes and management techniques.

The conversation bumped around for a while between the managers, and the frontline fell silent. As our patient integrator told us: "All *we* could think about was that the phone and intake for three disease centers were being covered by one person, who was undoubtedly getting swamped. And the meeting went on for another thirty minutes. So the progress we had made in the meeting was nullified. I think the managers thought we were a sullen bunch, by the end. And we certainly felt that for all their talk, they really didn't understand our jobs at all."

In Chapter 4, we focus more specifically on another act of sabotage—bringing up irrelevant issues, the specialty of the Tangent Talker—and zero in on the sins of Tangent Talkers and how to prevent them.

The Lost Talker

Ellen DeGeneres published a memoir in 1995 titled *My Point . . . And I Do Have One*. We don't think Ellen is a Lost Talker, but the title of her book nails the definition.

Lost Talkers start speaking with the best of intentions. They really do think that they have something meaningful to contribute to the conversation. But before too long (in fact, sometimes within thirty seconds or so), it becomes apparent that it's going to take them a while to figure out what that "something meaningful" is. Picture a snowball hurtling out of control down the side of a mountain, getting bigger as it goes. Somewhere in that snowball is a diamond. But to get it, you first have to stop the snowball. And then you have to dig. And dig.

Lost Talkers aren't Speech Saboteurs when they have a proven record for being insightful, and "lost" really means that they have a clearer grasp of the big picture and are "ahead of everyone else" in understanding it (which is why everyone else has a hard time following). In that case, staying with them to unravel their train of thought is going to bring a level of depth or awareness to the rest of the meeting's participants that they would not otherwise have had.

For example, consider Pam, a senior executive who was meeting with four other managers to decide on whether to adopt a new technology throughout their organization. Pam had prior experience and expertise with that technology, so when asked how it would be rolled out, she quickly got way ahead of the decision that was on the table and started to talk about the potential of the "next generation" technology, some two years into the future. Pam spoke for more than five minutes and finished up with a small laugh, saying, "I guess I took the long way around to articulate what really is a very simple point." One of the other executives in the meeting leaned forward, hand raised. "I'm sorry, Pam" he said. "Maybe I'm being dense, but what was that very simple point?" Everyone laughed, and Pam summed up by saying,

"This is the right move for us; it sets up well for the future." The meeting went on, with everyone just a little more in command of the big picture—and challenged to think more deeply about it—than before.

A Lost Talker also isn't a saboteur when "lost" means "inexperienced" and all of those present agree that it's worth spending a few minutes to help that person move up the learning curve—both for the Lost Talker and for the group. For example, take a junior supply chain manager who spends an inordinate amount of time delving into the specific technical details of a piece of equipment she needs to buy—unaware of the fact that her boss needs to know only whether the supplier will provide a piece of equipment that meets the technical needs of their company to approve the purchase.

Lost Talkers are Speech Saboteurs when they are chronic offenders. Or when it is increasingly clear that they have lost their train of thought but keep talking, trying to find it again. Or when listeners are as lost as the Lost Talker. Or when the listeners zone out or start furtively (or even openly) checking emails or texting other people (some of whom might even be in the meeting!).

The Sensitive Talker

Sensitive Talkers understand that people learn in different ways, and that just because they think they have explained something thoroughly doesn't mean that people get it—so they repeat their message or say the same thing in a different way so that everyone "gets it." Truly, this is a wonderful quality. The more scientists study the brain, the more they're finding out about the unique ways in which we all learn. And many times, Sensitive Talkers who sense that others might learn differently and therefore adapt their style as needed to reach all intended audiences, are a real gift to their group. The people who do this best tend to be able to offer multiple approaches to their listeners; their speeches are multifaceted and on point.

But when does this behavior cross the line into Sabotage by Speech? When Sensitive Talkers buy too fully into the idea that what is important enough to be said once is important enough to be said three times. When they inadvertently start to come across as condescending and people tune out because they're put off. When they are trying to accommodate everyone and end up wasting scarce group time.

As Professor Frank Cespedes of the Harvard Business School has said, "You don't always need to sell things twice."

Consider what happened at a meeting where participants were discussing how best to manage their organization's growing number of volunteers. One person described at length her vision for how the volunteers might be grouped and assigned tasks according to their interests, skills, age, and so forth. And then she simply began the same speech again, but this time, she drew pictures on a white board to accompany her talk. Finishing that description, she rewound and hit "play" again, pulling out a bag of Lego pieces from under the table and demonstrating the different groups by pushing together pieces of different sizes and colors.

"I learn visually," said one person who attended the meeting. "And so on one level, she really was helping me. But at some time I just wanted to say, 'Hey give me some credit for following through on my own if I don't get something.' This was a bit much. I mean, yes, her intentions were good. But it was a waste of our *collective* time."

The "Oh! Oh!" Talker

Remember the kid in fourth grade who always had his hand up in the air? The one who, every single time the teacher asked a question, would lean way out over his desk, grimace wildly, and whine "Oh! Oh!" until he (a) was called on and practically fell over himself giving his answer or opinion, or (b) was *not* called on and subsided, sighing and muttering to himself and maybe even rolling his eyes as the person the teacher *did* call on had his or her say?

If you have anyone like that in your meeting, maybe you're lucky. At their best, "Oh! Oh!" Talkers are like Hermione Granger of the Harry Potter books and movies. They know the topic inside and out, and they are the people who cut to the chase and save the group a lot of time by helping everyone home in quickly on what matters most. The speeches of "Oh! Oh!" Talkers often deliver the insight that people put to good use later on.

But "Oh! Oh!" Talkers can also be Speech Saboteurs. Sometimes, they feel the need to contribute to every conversation even when the discussion is not within the scope of their areas of expertise or knowledge. They talk so that people won't wonder why they're *not* talking, and they don't understand that they can come across as being ignorant by doing so. For example, if an "Oh! Oh!" Talker works in advertising, maybe he or she always chimes in with feedback on the creative direction of other people's projects, even when he or she is unfamiliar with the details and goals of those projects.

And sometimes, "Oh! Oh!" Talkers just parrot the comments of the people they feel are the most important participants at the meeting. They want to appear as if they are on top of the content, but since they're not, they feel safe in contributing an echo.

Unfortunately, these unwarranted contributions can take podium time from the people in the meeting whose voices *should* be heard.

The Jargonista

Jargonistas may be the least representative of the OSS tactic as it's written; nonetheless, it's an important ancillary form of Sabotage by Speech, particularly today.

Here's why: Jargonistas are often absolutely vital to the success of a group no matter what kind of group it is. That's because by virtue of either their age and experience or their youth and savvy, they have something unique and valuable to bring to the table. Maybe they are technical experts, sharing vital information about a work process. Maybe they are financial experts, delivering important messages about your budget or a new way of managing resources. Jargonistas are worth listening to. They will broaden your horizons.

But only if you understand them.

The problem with Jargonistas is that even if they don't commit Sabotage by Speech per se—even if they speak succinctly—they often fail to impart the information they believe they are passing along. They leave the meeting thinking they've told you something important, but you leave the meeting wondering what it was all about, or worse, thinking you've got the gist but missing a critical detail because you didn't understand it. The consequences show up later, when you, and the others on the receiving end of the Jargonistas' technical talk, make mistakes courtesy of the power of misinterpretation.

The sabotage, at its core, is committed because of an inability on the part of Jargonistas to recognize the needs of their audiences. They are off the mark from the first sentence, and so the more they talk (about technical details or what have you), the more confusion they sow.

For instance, when a seasoned COO tells the twenty-something marketing staff that "succeeding with this product requires a soup-to-nuts approach," those very smart young individuals may not have the faintest idea what their boss's boss's boss is talking about. (For those readers in the same boat, "soup to nuts" refers to a meal with many courses, beginning with soup and ending, probably hours later, with nuts. So "soup to nuts" is slang for "comprehensive" or "all inclusive" or "360-degree.")

On the other end of the spectrum, a tech-savvy twenty-something manager may tell an audience of people who don't even answer their own emails that "we can take full advantage of SMAC and really push right into this market." If you're lucky, someone will politely ask, "SMAC?" and the young manager will explain that SMAC stands for Social, Mobile, Analytics, and Cloud (technologies).

Speech Sabotage at the Group Level

You are likely to encounter any one of the six types of Speech Saboteurs in any working group. But sometimes Sabotage by Speech takes place at the group level. How is that possible?

If you've ever been at a meeting where the boss announces an unpopular decision or someone proposes a controversial plan or introduces a potentially cumbersome procedure, the meeting is followed by hush-hush conversations in people's offices or around the coffee machine or by emails flying back and forth debating the merits of the decision, the proposal, or the procedure, and so on, then you've experienced Sabotage by Speech at the group level.

We aren't talking about gossip—gossip is petty and personal. The "follow-up conversations" we are talking about can manifest as small venting or a healthy discussion among employees or group members who are invested in and even passionate about what's going on in their departments or groups. That's good. You want employees who care.

But these "conversations that keep on giving" can turn into deadly Sabotage by Speech. People can become so busy having side conversations or discussions in smaller groups after the large discussion or meeting that the conversations quickly spiral away from the issue that was on the table in the first place and the work that needs to get done. The conversations go off on tangents, and people follow them. Someone is misunderstood or misinterpreted, and people's feelings get hurt.

Sabotage by Speech at the group level is most likely to happen when there's a problem to be solved. Then everyone has a theory. Everyone becomes an expert. Everyone has a better solution—an alternative to the boss's decision, a stronger proposal, an improved procedure. When side conversations get out of hand—and people are not given a proper outlet or guidelines to voice their concerns or their opinions—then they can zap the productivity of the whole, undermine decisions, and create divisive factions.

At one multimillion-dollar charity, for example, a long series of meetings—discussing how to restructure the leadership team in the face of severe budget cuts—ended without resolution. This triggered a cloud of anxiety, with ensuing informal (and often furtive) conversations about personalities, management styles, favorites, the organization's mission and whether and how it should evolve, and succession planning. More people were drawn into the cloud each day, as members of the leadership team involved their direct reports. And the greater the buzz of commentary became, the less the leadership team was able to focus subsequent meetings on matching structure to budget. Eventually, two valuable members of the senior leadership team resigned, completely demoralized, before any resolution was reached.

The "speech that keeps on giving" isn't confined to the formal organization either. If you belong to a volunteer group, do you find that there are a lot of discussions-after-the-discussion? In a small kitchen area after the formal meeting? Via email? Does anyone's nose ever get put out of joint? Do you ever have to follow up with other private meetings to strategize how to get everyone working together again? That's Sabotage by Speech at the group level. The conversation keeps going and going behind the scenes, slowing down any meaningful resolution or action.

Fixing and Preventing Sabotage by Speech

The techniques to counter or remediate Sabotage by Speech in real time and to prevent it are pretty much the same. Some are more suited to address certain types of sabotage than others; we'll point out when that's the case.

Assign a Timekeeper

At the beginning of any group discussion, remind everyone how long the meeting is supposed to be and then appoint someone formally to keep track of time and interrupt people as needed. "That's great, Mary, but we should move on. We only have 20 minutes left." When someone makes that sort of comment off the cuff, it can come across as being hurtful. But if an official timekeeper says such a thing, everyone knows that this person is just doing his or her job.

You might also consider a "shot clock." We often use an old darkroom clock for the purpose in certain meeting settings. The sound it makes is so loud and obnoxious, there's no missing the message: Your time is up.

The shot clock is harsh but can be particularly useful for stopping Lost Talkers; not only will it keep them in check, but the technique may make them aware (for the first time) of how long it takes them to deliver their point—if they deliver one at all!

Provide a North Star

Give meeting participants something tangible—an agenda or specific goals—that you can all use to keep yourselves on track. Do this by communicating to participants—two days before a meeting, if you can—the purpose of the discussion and what you hope to resolve. Then, when you open the meeting, remind people of the goals by saying something like this: "What do we want to have decided, determined, discovered, or declared dead at the end of this meeting?"

By doing this, when people stray off topic, you can remind them of the meeting goals to help bring the discussion back to its original purpose. You will find that this tactic is particularly helpful to keep Tangent Talkers in check.

Invite the Right People

Write out your prospective list of attendees for the meeting or discussion and tailor it just as you would if you were deciding whom to invite to a barbeque—or a skydiving adventure. Think about who really needs to attend, why they're needed, and how they're going to benefit. Sometimes, people schedule meetings and invite the same people over and over out of habit. Sometimes, to be inclusive, they bring more voices to the table than are needed or useful. Drafting a guest list is a good discipline. When the only people in the room are there for a clear reason, and they know it, there's less of a chance that the Lost Talkers will get lost and the Tangent Talkers will ramble. There's more of a chance that the "Oh! Oh!" Talkers will participate for the right reasons, with the right information. And there's less of a chance of post-meeting angst.

Decide in Advance Whether You're Going to Ask for Comments and If So, Why

Sometimes, the sole purpose of a meeting is to have a group discussion or a brainstorming activity. That's fine. But too often, meeting leaders feel as if they should always open the floor for comments, no matter what the meeting was about, what its format was, or whether the goals have been met. The "politically correct" trend to ask for everyone to weigh in on everything isn't just human "water cooler" nature. It has been drummed into the heads of managers, especially human resource professionals, that employee involvement is critical. And sometimes, it's just not helpful.

For example, if you're at a meeting whose sole purpose is to dole out assignments, or you're in a large meeting where people have been asked to submit questions afterwards, then comments won't be welcome. There's no real purpose for them, and in reality, if you open up the floor for no reason, you're inviting the Long Talkers, Tangent Talkers, and Lost Talkers to party it up and wallow in their ability to commit Sabotage by Speech. It's important to defy the pressure to be inclusive, even if closing the meeting without an open-comment segment feels rude.

If you believe a comment session is needed at the end of a meeting, then we recommend following the "Two-Tap Rule," a technique we've adapted from volleyball. Make it clear that only two people can comment on (or "tap") each topic before you have to move on.

Finally, if you're running ahead of schedule, don't feel the need to open up a meeting for comments just because you have the time. Even if you've booked an hour for a meeting and you've spent only twenty minutes, stop. People will love to get any time bonus they can, and you won't run the risk of new topics being introduced, new decisions being made too quickly (Can't you hear the Tangent Talker saying, "We can squeeze this in; we have four minutes!"), and so forth. When you get to the end of a discussion, call it a day.

We also recommend steering clear of open-ended questions in general, such as, "Does anyone have any other comments?" In most cases, this leads directly to Sabotage by Speech, especially from the Tangent Talker. In order to prevent discussions from straying from the intended meeting agenda—or from continuing after the meeting has been called to a close— you might rephrase the question so it is focused on the issue at hand: "If you have any other comments about X, please let me know after the meeting."

A Goal and a Stretch

The sheer amount of data available to bring to bear on almost any topic these days can subtly encourage many types of Speech Saboteurs. To be effective contributors to meetings, people are often expected to be able to convert data into insight, and insight into *usable* insight, and there's real skill involved in doing that. It doesn't come naturally to most people.

You can help out (as a meeting leader, or as an attendee) by thinking about the information you're bringing to the table before you get there. How much are you expecting other people to know? How will they be able to use what you're putting in front of them to achieve the meeting's goals?

If you ask yourself these questions before you distribute or present materials, you'll be forcing yourself to stand in the other attendees' shoes. You will probably be able to tell whether you're expecting too much out of your colleagues, and whether what you want to contribute will be useful (and why, or why not). You may be able to keep yourself, and others, from committing Sabotage by Speech. (In particular, the "Oh! Oh!" Talkers will see clearly whether they have information that they ought to share. If they don't, those questions—along with a clear understanding of the reason their presence at the meeting is important—may at least give them the confidence they need to keep quiet.)

These questions might seem like overkill for small, informal groups. But you don't have to ask them formally, or fill out any sort of template, in order for them to be helpful. Considering them in the context of the purpose of your meeting should be enough. The goal in any meeting is to *foster usable insights that are then actually used to render a positive result*. Any meeting that does that has been a good meeting.

We don't think you should stop there, however. We think you should strive to generate usable insights, use them with positive results, and then *embed those insights into the organization so that the benefits repeat*. That's a stretch goal, sure, but if you meet it, our hats are off to you. You've certainly conquered Sabotage by Speech. It's rarefied ground, where saboteurs can't tread.

3

Sabotage by Committee

When possible, refer all matters
to committees, for "further study
and consideration." Attempt to
make the committees as large as
possible—never less than five.

hen this tactic was published in 1944, "committee" was pretty much the only word most
people used for a working group. Today, we
have "work teams," "initiatives," "task forces," and
lots of other names for people working together on
a project. Such groups are important, whatever you
call them, and it's safe to say that without them, necessary work wouldn't get done.

Sometimes a piece of work requires the efforts of more than one person, but a permanent organization doesn't make sense. So a temporary workgroup is assembled around a task—a committee of some kind. Or conversely, a larger group decides that a task doesn't require everyone's efforts; a subgroup can take care of it. Again—a committee is the answer.

Consider a high school dance. You don't need the entire PTA to help the kids get organized. You don't need everyone to scout and book a location (or reserve the gym and alert the janitors), decorate, make food, arrange for chaperones, keep an eye on safety issues, and attend to the dozen-other-things that need to get done before, during, and after the big event. But you do need all of those things to happen. So you ask people to volunteer for committees—the food committee, the decorating committee, the cleanup committee, and so on. The work is broken up into manageable chunks.

Committees are often very good things—in fact, in a few other places in this book, we actually recommend that a committee be formed. But committees also can be fertile grounds for Sabotage by Committee.

For starters, committees represent the possibility for accountability to be lost. When a larger group delegates something to a committee, control of the task or activity goes off the radar of the group's leader. (In the case of the high school dance, that leader would be the head of the PTA.) Many times, committees are left to devise their own ground rules, which can mean that the committee never bothers to set *any* rules.

Often, no one is explicitly made head of the committee, and so no one is responsible for the work of the committee getting done. In such a scenario, committee meetings can be fraught with arguments. Feelings get hurt, miscommunications occur . . . and the work doesn't get done as well as it should. In the worst-case scenario, the committee stops its work because no one feels empowered even to call a meeting.

When an individual is delegated a task, someone is clearly in charge. But if the work is too large for a single person and a temporary committee is formed, that accountability may be diluted or lost completely. A person's job becomes a committee's job, which sometimes can mean it's no one's job—with similar negative outcomes.

Clear sabotage. But that's not all. As our friends in the OSS no doubt understood only too well, committees, by their very nature, have tunnel vision. Once they are formed around a mandate, they often find it difficult to change course in the middle of their work—even if a change is warranted.

Say a neighborhood committee is formed to design a playground for an empty lot in a run-down area of town. The members are well organized; they name a leader and start to work, researching different types of playground equipment, looking into prices, and so forth. One day, they find out that the city is going to put up a large housing complex for senior citizens adjacent to that empty lot. On a map, it's clear that the proposed playground will be separated from the rest of the neighborhood by this housing complex.

Most likely, the committee nonetheless will continue on with the task of designing the playground. Why? Because it is the "design a playground" committee, not the "what to do with an empty lot" committee. Maybe the members even have some expertise in designing playgrounds—but no expertise in designing, say, a community garden or a handicapped-accessible landscape designed to attract birds or butterflies, which might be better ideas for the empty lot at this point. They doggedly continue designing the playground because that's the reason the committee was created.

Finally, committees . . . can be . . . sluggishly . . . slow. (This third quality is probably what was so alluring to the OSS.) Many committees are formed without clear deadlines. Their task is to study something or to come up with a recommendation of some sort. No one really knows at the outset what it will take to do this work well. So there is no deadline. Maybe there's a hoped-for "delivery" date, but sometimes, a committee doesn't even have that.

What's more, the work of the committee isn't front and center for its members. Take the high school dance again. Some of the committee members are teachers. Their committee work will have to get in line behind their teaching, their after-school activities, their families, and their other commitments. Ditto with parent members. Day jobs, anyone? Kids? (Of course—that's why they're in the PTA.) Aging parents? Committee work is rarely *urgent*. And so it gets put off.

Ben, a volunteer bartender at events at his synagogue, knows this particularly well. In fact, he used it once to his advantage, in a deliberate (and successful) effort to commit Sabotage by Committee.

In the early 2000s, an important national organization was moved to deal with the issue of alcohol use in the Jewish community. A letter went out urging synagogues to stop serving liquor at the various social affairs held in their buildings.

Ben's rabbi called him into his office and showed him the letter. "Ben," he said, "We're going to need to deal with this."

Ben knew the congregation had to be responsive to the request—but he also knew that he and other volunteer bartenders had already dealt with the possibility of alcohol abuse in their small community in an appropriate way, and that spending more time on the national organization's initiative would be a waste of time and energy. So he said: "Rabbi, we should have a committee. And not just a few of us— but a broad representation: people who help with the

youth, with the men's and women's groups, some
board members, perhaps a local caterer. You should
be on it too. I'll ask the other bartenders, and a few of
the physicians and psychologists from the community who can add a scientific perspective. We should
take a sweeping look at *all* alcohol use in our synagogue and our community at large and emerge with
a comprehensive alcohol-use policy covering *every*
type of event and situation."

"Great idea," the rabbi responded. "A committee
it is."

You may be able to guess the punch line. The committee never met, and the situation at Ben's synagogue
is exactly the same as it was before the letter arrived.
The issue of alcohol use in the Jewish community is
no longer in the national organization's spotlight. No
action taken; apparently no action needed.

The best way to stop an idea dead in its tracks
without actually having to disagree with anything
is to assign it to a committee—preferably one, like
Ben's suggested committee, with a diverse member-
ship, no clear objectives, and no deadlines.

Ben was the saboteur—purposefully, because he
knows how this sort of Sabotage by Committee works.
He knows that committees can be the black holes of
an organization—issues go in, but never come out.
And he didn't want his congregation to have to deal
with something that he felt strongly was a nonissue for

them, since he and the other bartenders had already taken over responsibility for the storage and serving of alcohol at their synagogue functions.

Nobody would ever spot the sabotage—because if anyone were to ask the rabbi what his congregation was doing about the matter, he could truthfully say that a committee had been formed to study it.

No harm, no foul? Maybe, in this case. At least from Ben's point of view. But we would wager that most committees are not formed with the intention of deliberately scuttling an idea. In many cases, people form committees with a positive intent to study something more carefully. They want to be sure they make the right decision in the end, and so they ask for a group of people to examine the issue closely.

But in some cases, committees keep things from happening, and that can be highly destructive.

Spotting Sabotage by Committee

We can usually sniff out a committee that doesn't work a mile away. Luckily for us all, you can too. It's actually fairly easy to tell if a committee may be a source of sabotage. Here are the telltale signs.

Committee Members Can't
Seem to Agree

The members talk a lot and debate a lot, but nothing is ever resolved and no one takes charge.

Organizations are complicated, and most of the time groups of people work together to solve problems. But who *owns* the problem? Who, ultimately, is accountable for resolving the problem? If a committee has been formed, the answer can't be the person who delegated the work—"the head of the PTA" or "the boss." That's too broad. It has to be someone *on* the committee, even if the committee is made up of equals from different departments or areas.

If no single person ultimately has accountability for resolving an issue or coming to closure, then there's a good chance the group is an unsuspecting victim of inadvertent Sabotage by Committee.

There's No Specific Plan or Goal

If no one has articulated what the outcome of the committee's work is—a report, a recommendation, an action—then the committee is in trouble.

It's like giving a high school student a broad topic for independent study (such as "comedy in the twentieth century"), with no guidance on what elements are expected, how the final work product should be presented, or what criteria will be used for grading. The odds are that the final product won't be very good.

At one company we know, the executives seem to love committee work. They spend all day rushing from one working-group meeting to the next. "Busy" means "valued." People whose calendars don't have any daylight appearing on them for weeks in advance must be very important. But they don't seem to accomplish much at any particular meeting.

As one of the company's leaders told us: "Around here, a good meeting means we all like each other a little more at the end of the meeting. Nothing may have been accomplished, but we feel like we had a good conversation, worked well together, and know each other better as a result of the time we just spent. And a *great* meeting is a good meeting with donuts!"

Happy times, happy times. But results? Maybe not. Wasted time? Probably.

There's No Deadline

Although certain work has a tight deadline—a product launch, for example—much of the effort of modern organizations seems to drift along at its own pace. Either there's a clear and immediate deadline and everyone knows it—"We need to have the business plan in front of the Investment Committee a week from Tuesday"—or the deadline is vague—"We might have something ready toward the end of the next quarter."

Some tasks are too complex to know in advance when the work will be completed. In those cases, interim milestones are often established instead—"We need a work plan in ninety days."

But if there's no due date or interim milestones, then chances are good that a committee is going to be ineffective. Either the task won't be taken seriously and the committee won't meet regularly, or when it does meet the work will drift along without a drive to closure. Deadlines provide focus, and without focus it's hard for a committee to get things done.

Making Committees Work

A few simple fixes can transform committees from becoming sources of Sabotage by Committee to being productive, collaborative tools.

Fix 1: Determine Roles at the Outset, with Particular Care to Assigning Accountability

All three of the issues just discussed—no mechanism to close on an agreement, no goals, and no deadlines—have a common root cause: Nobody is in charge. Or at least nobody feels they are both "on the hook" for the outcome and empowered to the point that they can step forward and clarify goals, set and hold deadlines, and drive agreement among the committee members.

In the world of project management, a simple but highly effective model for discussing accountability has been invented. It's called RACI. If you're familiar with RACI, you can just skip the next few paragraphs. If not, you're about to learn a simple technique that will become one of the most powerful tools in your personal management arsenal—and a great tool to prevent Sabotage by Committee.

Let's say a task needs to be performed, such as deciding whether to expand a restaurant chain into a new state. The Boss has decided to assign people to a committee that will look into the situation. The Region Head clearly needs to be represented. Restaurant Operations wants someone there, since ultimately they have to run the new restaurants. Marketing should be represented as well, since there are all kinds of implications for promoting the new locations. Procurement? Of course. New suppliers would have to be lined up. Finance? Someone has to figure out whether the new restaurants will make a profit. Human Resources? New employees will need to be hired. Real Estate? New locations will have to be identified and secured. IT? Those new restaurants will need technological systems. Legal? Contracts will be involved. Franchise Relations? Internal Communications? So far we've got eleven people who could potentially belong in this committee, and more groups and functions will want to get on board once the review gains momentum.

But are all eleven necessary? Do we really want to juggle eleven individual calendars every time the committee wants to schedule a meeting?

That's where RACI comes in. Under the RACI model, members of a group can hold one of four roles:

R Responsible

A Accountable

C Consulted

I Informed

In the case of the restaurant chain committee, each of the department representatives would have one of these four roles assigned to him or her. Let's take Marketing. Since market analysis, advertising and promotional costs, and competitive dynamics will all factor into this decision of whether to expand the chain into a new state, it's clear that the Marketing Department will need to have a representative on the committee. That would make Marketing an

"R"—that is, one of the functions *responsible* for the decision and therefore a necessary member of the committee.

Is the same true of Legal though? Does the representative from Legal need to be at every meeting and in the loop on every element of the decision? Probably not. In all likelihood, Legal only needs to be *consulted* before any actions with legal implications are taken. So Legal is assigned a "C" role. The person from Legal doesn't need to be on the committee as long as he or she is consulted about those aspects of the decision that have a legal implication *before* those decisions get made.

How about IT? This role won't come into play until a decision is moving toward execution, and the IT people won't have a bearing on the "yes or no" of the decision itself. But they need to be in the loop. They need to be *informed,* but it's okay for the committee to inform them *after* a recommendation or decision gets made. So they can be assigned an "I" role.

That leaves one critical role left to be assigned. The "Accountable" role.

Although the Boss is ultimately accountable for everything that happens in the organization (remember President Harry Truman's famous desktop sign, "The Buck Stops Here"?), if the Boss wants to leverage her organization, she needs to delegate accountability—to make other people the owners of various decisions. The alternative is for her to own them all, which will ultimately limit the capability of the company to function effectively or grow.

Decisions need owners, and a committee can't be an owner. A *person* needs to be the owner. And so a person needs to be delegated the authority to be in charge of the final decision of the committee. Not forever, not without review, not without the ability of the Boss to step in and challenge or even overrule the decision. But of the members of the committee, one individual needs to be singled out as *accountable*—the "A" role in RACI. That person ultimately owns the work of the team and owns the recommendation.

Many organizations are squeamish about assigning accountability to a single person. Politics and personalities are involved. If the Region Head owns the process of deciding whether to expand into a new state, does that mean that he or she can force the decision in a direction that Marketing doesn't like? What if Operations feels they don't have adequate capacity to support the move? Wouldn't it be better if the group made the decision together?

Of course it would. And of course they might. And if that's how it works out—with everyone joining hands in unanimous glory singing "Kumbaya"—that would be a terrific outcome. And the Boss would, of course, much rather have a unanimous recommendation than a committee that ends up feuding.

But decisions can be messy. Trade-offs need to be made. There could be perceived winners and losers. And unless the Boss wants all those messy decisions to end up on her desk, they need to be put on someone else's desk—the person with the "A" role in the RACI framework who ultimately owns the most successful possible outcome of the committee's work.

Using RACI to great effect involves remembering just four phrases: Responsible—*the team*. Accountable—*one person*. Consulted—*before* a decision is made. Informed—*after* a decision is made.

The clarity provided by the RACI model can transform your organization's committees overnight, so it's worth taking the time to learn and practice this simple technique.

Fix 2: Make Sure the Task Requires a Committee

We used to joke with the senior management team of one of our clients that they dealt with issues ranging from massive world-scale acquisitions to the location for the annual company picnic. One team member told us, "Not only do we talk about where to hold the picnic, but last year we talked about whether the children of non-spouse significant others should be included as guests."

These issues aren't unimportant. But a senior management team probably doesn't need to deal with them. The best organizations, and the best leaders, make sure that the task fits the team and that committees are formed only when they are needed.

Many decisions benefit from multiple points of view, but it's important to ask three questions:

> Is this issue "committee-worthy"?
>
> Is discussing this issue the highest and best use of these people's time together?
>
> Is this an extraordinary decision that needs to be outside the bounds of someone's job description?

If the answer to any of these questions is "no," then you might need to consider whether, for instance, the issue can be delegated to a single accountable person, or whether it could be part of someone's regular job responsibilities.

Fix 3: Keep Committees as Small as Possible

Jeff Bezos, the chairman, CEO, and founder of Amazon.com, once said that if you can't feed a team with two pizzas, the team is too large.[1] The same is true of committees.

There's also empirical proof, in the form of a study commissioned by the *Wall Street Journal*, that this is the case with at least one special kind of committee: the boards of directors of publicly traded corporations.[2]

Boards exhibit some of the classic characteristics of the toughest committees to manage. While they have a chairperson, members aren't that individual's subordinates. Members' votes are equal. The mandate of a public company board is in some ways quite specific and in other ways broad and undefined. They also come in various sizes. The average board is composed of somewhere between ten and twelve directors, but some are smaller and some are larger.

The *Wall Street Journal* study investigated one simple issue: Do corporations with smaller boards (eight to ten directors) show a difference in performance from those with larger boards (twelve to fourteen directors)?

To answer that question, researchers looked at returns of nearly four hundred companies with market capitalization of more than $10 billion from 2011 to 2014. The results? Companies with smaller than average boards (an average of 9.5 members) *outperformed* their peers across ten industry segments by 8.5 percent, while companies with larger than average boards (an average of 14 members) *underperformed* their industry peers by 10.85 percent.

Smaller boards meant that each director could be more personally involved in decisions. With larger boards, points in discussion were repeated more often, and it was harder to "dig in" with a second or third follow-up question. Board members would state their points of view or ask a question, but discussions tended to be more formal. With the smaller boards, members engaged in more interactive dialogue, having genuine conversations that probed more deeply into specific topics. Smaller meant more "hands on," and larger meant more distant.

The addition of just a few committee members can turn a small, effective, nimble, invested team into a lumbering, indecisive, distant group of overseers. And this can happen easily and naturally when "just one more" person volunteers (or volunteers someone else). But "more" means "less" when it comes to committees, so saying "no" when you have a quorum can drive a dramatic outcome in group effectiveness.

There's a reason why the OSS recommended making committees as large as possible. They knew that larger committees were inherently less effective and would grind down the productivity of organizations. Keep committees small and nimble to prevent them from becoming breeding grounds of Sabotage by Committee.

Fix 4: Control Who Serves on Important Committees

The most common way to populate a committee is to ask for volunteers. That's because being on a committee generally represents an effort above and beyond a person's regular job. So if someone volunteers, that person is acknowledging that he or she can make room in their schedule to take on another responsibility. While that may be the easiest way to get a committee going, it is often not the best way. Those volunteers may not be the right people to get the job done.

Here's a useful committee model from the nonprofit world: the "Four Ws." For someone to make a good committee member, he or she should fill one (or more) of four functions: be a good Worker, provide Wisdom, contribute Wealth, or be Window-Dressing that will increase the stature of the committee.

> **Worker:** The committee candidate has a good grasp of what actions will need to follow any decision. This person will be involved in carrying out those actions and will provide the time and attention needed to get the required tasks done.

> **Wisdom:** The committee candidate will be able to apply sound judgment or to spot trouble around the corner (having been around that corner, or a similar one, before). Wisdom is about having the ability to recognize patterns and to make connections where others might not—abilities that come from years of experience.

Wealth: The committee candidate has access to needed resources—and that doesn't mean just money in this context. Setting up an obstacle course that features big tires for a high school field day will be much easier if the obstacle course committee includes someone who works at a tire store. A committee that is exploring venues for a concert would benefit from having someone in the group who performs music regularly and understands acoustics. Wealth can also mean a person who has connections or relationships to others with a desired expertise or influence.

Window-Dressing: The committee candidate lends extra credibility by virtue of his or her associations outside of the committee. For example, a committee studying school breakfasts for kindergarteners would benefit from having the head of the nutrition department at the local college involved.

In going through the RACI process while staffing a committee, it's useful to have the Four Ws in mind as well. Are enough Workers members of the team (Responsible)? If you have folks who will be serving as Window-Dressing, is it okay to have them Consulted or Informed rather than members of the team itself?

Often, we see nonprofit boards of twenty, thirty, or more people—way too large for any real work to get done. The board members may be large contributors (Wealth) or may have been Workers in the past but haven't contributed for some time. In these cases, we advise splitting the board into an advisory board and a managing or executive board. An advisory board might be Consulted or Informed but isn't necessarily viewed as the team Responsible for running the group. That role falls to the smaller executive board or managing board.

The Four Ws and RACI make a great combination in configuring a committee for maximum effectiveness.

Another best practice to move from a volunteer-based committee to a well-designed and well-balanced committee is to split committee formation into two stages. Ask for volunteers or nominees, without committing to anyone at that point. Use RACI to define what role those individuals should have. Then, in private, put together the committee you think is best for the job. To follow through, circle back to those people you didn't select and let them know that you appreciate their interest but you have enough volunteers. Or ask them to serve on a different group, if that's appropriate. Or give them roles that will have them be Consulted or Informed, but don't make them Responsible members of the committee itself.

Fix 5: Set Clear Deliverables and Deadlines and Require Periodic, Written Progress Updates

Many committees are "standing" committees—permanent groups that generate options, preferences and/or decisions on a periodic basis. The Town School Committee meets monthly to consider new questions or issues that are brought up as needed. The company's Risk Management Committee meets quarterly. The Board's Audit Committee meets with the outside auditors semi-annually.

But most committees are set up to tackle a specific question or topic. And those types of committees can, if left on their own, continue indefinitely with no clear work product. They just meet, without a clear destination or time frame.

The special-purpose committee or task force can be a huge sinkhole of personal and organizational time and energy. At some of our client organizations, executives dash from meeting to meeting all day long—and it's hard to see, at the end of the week, a tangible outcome commensurate with the effort they've expended.

Governments, in an effort to prevent this type of organizational drift, often enact "sunset" provisions. These rules say that a committee or activity will continue for a set period of time. At the end of that time, the group needs to be proactively renewed—otherwise, it fades out of existence like a sunset.

But sunset provisions are rare in the private and nonprofit worlds. Committees, task forces, initiatives—all of these can drift on for weeks, months, or years. They move forward just enough to claim to still be "in business" but not enough to come to a definitive result and work themselves out of a job.

Try this simple fix. Either set a deadline, if you created or chair a committee, or ask for a deadline, if you're a committee member. Set a clear outcome, or "deliverable," that needs to be ready by that deadline. Or if you're not in a position to set a deliverable, at least ask that you be given one. And set up a pattern of regular reports, written if possible, documenting what's been achieved and what lies ahead. Or ask that such reports be built in to the committee's activities and expectations.

This sounds simple, but it's surprising how often this sort of thing doesn't happen. The potential for Sabotage by Committee is extremely high. It's not that a committee will end up with the wrong outcome; it's that people will meet . . . and meet . . . and meet. And a great meeting will be a good meeting with donuts, regardless of whether real progress is made.

A Most Potent Tool for Saboteurs

Committees can be deadly when they have the appearance that work is taking place when in fact very little is happening. They give people and tasks the look of productivity, masking inaction and zapping energy away from real work. They can be potent nests of potential sabotage because of their unique ability to suck energy out of an organization.

So while being vigilant about the makeup and purpose of committees might seem like tedious work—after all, if you are delegating a decision to a committee, it's likely because you don't have the time to deal with that decision yourself—it is well worth the extra care. Applying basic techniques such as RACI and the Four Ws more than pays off in helping an organization stay productive and sabotage-free.

4

Sabotage by Irrelevant Issues

Bring up irrelevant issues as
frequently as possible.

Some of the people who bring up irrelevant
issues—whether in one-on-one conversations
or in meetings—do it blatantly: They take
every opportunity they can to inject random stories
into conversations that are supposed to be about
something else. These are the people who are always
saying things like, "You know, that reminds me of
the time when . . ." They're pretty easy to spot, and
when their banter starts to waste too much time,
they're pretty easy to shut down.

They're not your saboteurs. And in fact, most
of the time our personal anecdotes, tangents, and

digressions are good ones. They refresh the conversation, like taking a minute to stand up and stretch when you've been sitting down for a long time. They form the foundations of the personal connections that make us want to work with each other, that help us create strong teams. We *do* want to hear about our colleague's puppy. We *do* want to hear about the wonderful restaurant our boss found in Chicago on her last trip—especially if we're heading there soon. We probably *don't* want a 20-minute discourse in the middle of a time-sensitive conversation on something else. But yes, we want to know these things! And if someone does run on, well, as we said, it's usually easy to interrupt with a simple, "Hey I really want to hear about that, but later, okay? We have to get this done."

The people who commit Sabotage by Irrelevant Issues are doing something completely different. They are experts at deception. That is, they make people think they're doing one thing when they're really doing something else. (Magicians should be envious.) Saboteurs make you think that what they're talking about is relevant and important when in reality what they're saying is tangential, unimportant, or even inappropriate. They don't know they're doing it, so their earnestness and honesty help make their case. And the people on the receiving end are instantly, innocently swept off course because they believe what they think they see or hear.

Sabotage by Irrelevant Issues instigates a real tangle of damage not just by wasting time, but also by sending people off in different directions, with different perceptions of priorities, problems, and processes. It's a catalyst for unnecessary tension and eroding relationships, as each person tries to make sense of the group discussion but finds it harder and harder to understand where the common ground lies or what the common goal is.

That's why understanding how to stop this kind of sabotage is so important.

Like an Optical Illusion

Sabotage by Irrelevant Issues often starts when someone is trying to make a *comparison* between the issues at hand and something that occurred in the past. They may do so to make a point, like "Let's learn from our mistakes," or "Let's learn from others' mistakes." But what happens in such situations is that too often the other people present will assume that the comparison is relevant without stopping to figure out if it's apples and oranges instead.

Usually, these comparisons are paragons of either disaster or virtue, and they involve competitors. For example, at a local high school PTA meeting that begins with a discussion of how many chaperones should be at the prom, a person might throw in a comparison like, "When the Pierce School held its after-prom party, they really messed up. Their chaperones were all grouped in one corner of the room, and I heard they left two exits unattended." Never mind that the meeting's intent was to discuss the prom, not the after-prom party, or that the Pierce School is notorious for wild parties, while the local high school is known for its low-key dances.

By comparing the school prom to another prom-related incident that had a very different set of variables, the Irrelevant Issues Saboteur sparked a heated discussion over big-picture concerns such as whether an after-prom party should be allowed or whether there should even be a prom at all. The meeting got off track and became a fiasco.

Another way in which inadvertent saboteurs might bring up irrelevant issues is by introducing a *burning issue*. Irrelevant Issues Saboteurs usually bring the burning issue into a conversation fully believing that they are going to save the day by calling attention to a topic that deserves critical attention. In a meeting to discuss the company's extended warranty program, for example, someone might say, "I just saw the latest survey results about customer service, and we have a problem that we need to talk about right now." The conversation then turns to the quality of customer service—despite the fact that the meeting is not about general customer service issues. Since no one is prepared to talk about customer service, the discussion degenerates into unproductive bickering. Meanwhile, the extended warranty issue gets short shrift, and the group overlooks an important aspect of why it was meeting to begin with.

Sometimes, the inadvertent Irrelevant Issues Saboteur brings up irrelevant issues by calling for information about a *side issue*. Consider this example: Five volunteers are planning an awards dinner for the local branch of a national service organization. Everyone is focused on picking a theme except for Dan, who isn't really paying attention. He has something on his mind that he feels is more important than picking a theme. Dan's son-in-law has just been named manager of a conference center in the next town, and he sees an opportunity to help his relative. So out of the blue, Dan says, "You know, we really need to think more about the venue we're renting before we plan the theme for this awards dinner."

His fellow volunteers look at him in admiration. "He's right!" they think. "Dan's the Man! How can we possibly settle on a theme without knowing what the venue looks like, and what its restrictions might be regarding decorations, music, and food service?"

The problem is, none of those other volunteers realize that Dan is doing something we call "forum shopping"—looking for supporters for his own agenda. And if just one more inadvertent Irrelevant Issues Saboteur brings up a side issue—suppose Mary's best friend's daughter works at a competing venue—the conversation's original purpose might just suffer death by a thousand cuts.

Preventing and Addressing Sabotage by Irrelevant Issues

Dealing in the moment with Sabotage by Irrelevant Issues is extremely difficult if you haven't taken steps to prepare to keep it at bay. In the heat of a conversation, particularly during a meeting, this kind of sabotage can fly under the radar, and by the time you spot it happening, it's too late to refocus the discussion on the original topic. The following tips will help you avoid Sabotage by Irrelevant Issues in the first place, and spot it and deflect it in the moment if it happens anyway.

Common Focus and Goal

Articulate explicitly and clearly a common focus and a common goal for the discussion or meeting. Keep it posted front and center. Oliver Wendell Holmes Sr. once said, "I would not give a fig for the simplicity this side of complexity, but I would give my life for the simplicity on the other side of complexity." Clarity is the "simplicity on the other side of complexity."

Say you're the head of customer experience at an online retailer, and you've called a meeting because you want to "transform the customer experience." Do the meeting's attendees know why the process needs to be transformed? Do they have any idea what you think "transformation" entails? They need to know these things before the meeting so they can be thinking about what they will bring to the table.

If attendees don't know the focus and goal of the meeting, they may bring up issues or introduce information that they believe to be helpful when in fact it's not. The head of the department might have considered sharing a more explicit direction for the meeting by providing the following information in advance: "The costs of our current approach have been steadily increasing. Let's meet to discuss how we can change the processes in our department to save money while keeping the high-quality customer experience for which we're known."

It's not always possible to clarify the purpose of a meeting or group discussion beforehand. In such cases, devote the first part of the meeting or discussion to nailing down the common focus. When you're holding a meeting or discussion to kick off a project or tackle a challenge, it's even more critical that you set aside time to come to an agreement, as a group, about the purpose and focus of both that meeting and the project or challenge.

As Jeffrey Flaks, COO of Hartford HealthCare, a large Connecticut hospital system serving several million patients, told us: "There's an almost magical moment that occurs when you're working on the early stages of a problem and someone in the group puts their finger on it in an unbelievably succinct fashion. Sometimes it's just a phrase. Sometimes it's just a sentence or even two. But there's an almost palpable acknowledgment around the room when people land on a common definition of the problem."

Once you have that common definition, it's a lot easier to see when someone is straying off point and unwittingly sabotaging your group.

Understand and Explain the Implications of Your Group's Activities

Irrelevant issues often creep into a discussion when someone asks (or complains) about how something will affect them when, in truth, it won't.

So before going into a meeting, you need to make sure you're aware of the implications of your group's activities. Chart them. Put them on a simple template, or make a graphic. Even if your map isn't fully filled out, you must begin that process in advance. That way, when someone asks, "But what about my people? How will this affect them?" or when someone complains, "This decision is totally going to screw up my other team's plans," you will be ready to respond.

Suppose, for example, you are in charge of marketing and public relations for an athletic league. Half of the teams' names, determined decades ago, sound too politically incorrect for today's standards. You know that if you don't make a move to change the names this year, the backlash will probably damage the league significantly. So you come up with new names and get the requisite approvals from the head of the league and the other top managers. But then, when you have the floor to announce the changes to the organization at large, a few people loudly object.

If one of those people says, "We've already ordered the uniforms and the cups and other doodads for the concession stand! Do you know how much we'll have to pay to redo everything?" then that person has raised a relevant issue that you'll have to deal with.

But suppose the person speaking up objects to the new names on the grounds that the parties that were most offended by the old names should have been asked to weigh in on the decision, and that the new names will also affect ancillary businesses that have capitalized on the league in the past.

If you've got clarity on the problem at hand, and you're aware of the "reach" of your activities on other parts of the organization, you'll see that this is an attempt at Sabotage by Irrelevant Issues. Yes, the objector's intentions are good, but you will know that the issue is irrelevant to the discussion at hand, and you'll be able to say: "No, what we're doing should not have any bearing on that. That's a topic for another meeting."

Set the Pace, the Form, and the Process

Before or at the beginning of any meeting of size (more than about seven people), define and/or review the ground rules of the conversation: How long will the meeting be? How long do you plan to spend on each issue? Will the meeting be formal or informal? Who is expected to speak? Some very well run organizations we know actually post the answers to these questions on the walls of their conference rooms.

If you don't do this, you may find that the experience turns out like an ill-planned road trip. You're all in your cars heading north, but some of you are on the highway while others are taking the scenic route.

Setting ground rules is different from defining the purpose of a meeting because setting rules deals with form. Many regularly scheduled meetings have unspoken rules about form. For example, there's the lunchroom meeting—in some companies, an informal gathering used to brainstorm. All are welcome. Then there's the "end of day" check-in—often a quick, superefficient, no-side-topics-tolerated meeting just to confirm what's done and what's left to do on a given project before everyone runs to catch their trains. Your own organization may have a variety of "norms" for certain types of meetings. New people learn them quickly (they're stared down when they violate an unspoken rule), and Sabotage by Irrelevant Issues is rare.

But meetings that aren't part of the regular flow of business are vulnerable to sabotage because the form isn't always clear. Your intent might be to get through seven agenda items quickly, but other people may see the time as an opportunity to connect with colleagues they haven't seen in a while. Your intent might be to get one decision made and then spend time sharing insights about another topic, while other people may view the meeting as an opportunity to make several other decisions too. Sabotage by Irrelevant Issues loves the vague.

Priorities matter. Guidelines matter. There's a time and a place for digressions—be clear about what that time and place is.

Create a Template for Progress

When you are working regularly with a group to accomplish a goal, or for a limited period of time to complete a discreet complex task or a project with multiple steps, it's helpful to keep track of what needs to happen, by what date, and who needs to tackle each task. A template for progress is the schedule that keeps you on track from milestone to milestone. It dictates what you need to cover in *this* conversation versus the *next* conversation, and it helps you keep moving forward, as opposed to backwards or sideways. It makes you less vulnerable to Sabotage by Irrelevant Issues because everyone present knows what needs to be accomplished *right now*.

For groups that have a particular goal or end date in mind, it also makes sense to create a timetable—a project plan—with the goal clearly stated, the end date clearly marked, and a list of major tasks that need to be completed, by which date, along the way. A simple spreadsheet should do the trick. Again, this is a simple mechanism designed to keep everyone on track. It's also something that meeting participants can point to if they think someone else is committing Sabotage by Irrelevant Issues. A written schedule, a written plan—these tools can "take the blame" when someone wants to cut off a would-be saboteur.

Tap Someone to Be the
Content Referee

Another helpful technique to keep people from de-railing your group's focus and conversations is to assign a content referee for every meeting. This person intervenes when anyone brings up an irrelevant issue—such as flawed comparisons, burning issues, and side issues—and redirects the conversation to the agreed-upon common focus.

In Chapter 2 we suggested having a timekeeper to prevent Long Talkers and others from committing Sabotage by Speech. The content referee has a similar role but focuses on content rather than time. If your meeting is large enough to accommodate a timekeeper and a referee, it is best to keep these roles separate. Doing so keeps one person from shouldering all the pressure for keeping the meeting on track. (Being the "bad cop" isn't easy!) But for most medium or small meetings, it probably makes sense to combine the two jobs.

By appointing a content referee, you're giving everyone permission to raise whatever issues they feel are relevant. You're sending the messages that input is welcome and people don't need to fear speaking up. If they accidentally bring up issues that are irrelevant, the referee can redirect the conversation. If the referee intervenes, it doesn't mean that another topic isn't important; it just may not be relevant to the issue being discussed at that particular moment. (This is where the next tip, the "parking lot," comes into play.)

One caution: Unless your group is super small (fewer than five people), don't make the boss the content referee. That person has too much skin in the game, and others may be reluctant to speak up if the person in charge wields the authority of the referee, too.

Open a "Parking Lot"

A "parking lot," where irrelevant issues can be placed for consideration at another time, is the content referee's best friend. This tip helps avoid "shoot the messenger" syndrome by deflecting blame away from the person who is pointing out the sabotage while at the same time offering a useful venue where people raising side or other irrelevant issues can have their say.

If someone raises an irrelevant issue, the content referee can put it in the parking lot by saying: "I understand what you're saying / it's clear you have a lot of passion about it—but let's put it in the parking lot and address it before we leave / take it up at another meeting. This isn't the time or place/group for this discussion." Creating a parking lot for irrelevant issues allows inadvertent Irrelevant Issues Saboteurs to save face. Their thoughts are respected; they've just been redirected to air them at a more appropriate time, in a more appropriate place.

However, the content referee needs to be careful in designating when and where people will be given the stage to bring up their issues. Beware of putting too many things in the parking lot and inviting people who raised the irrelevant issues to bring them up at the end of a meeting. Maybe some people can be excused from the meeting before you circle back to this topic. Maybe it's better aired in a conversation with one person after the meeting.

But if you put something in the parking lot, make no mistake: You have to follow up on it one way or another. Someone who has been "parked" once and then ignored may get resentful and withhold information in the future. Then you've got a deliberate saboteur on your hands.

Watch Out for Apples-to-Oranges Comparisons

We used an example of apples-to-oranges comparisons early on in the chapter. Consider it again here. Suppose you say, "Hey, I'm the tallest person here!" Well, maybe you are, but is that information relevant? Not if you're the tallest seven-year-old in the room, your goal is to play for the Los Angeles Lakers, and you don't know the rules of professional basketball.

Knowing whether someone is raising an "apples to apples" or an "apples to oranges" issue is a big part of figuring out whether you're looking at relevant information or are being hit by potential Sabotage by Irrelevant Issues.

Consider, for example, what it might cost a company to recruit employees. One global energy company recently calculated that it was costing approximately $50,000 to hire one person. That's an absolute number, and maybe it sounds reasonable. But is it?

How does that number sound relative to what the company paid to hire someone five years ago? Well, if the company used to pay $65,000 to hire someone, then that's a significant improvement. But is *that* information relevant? Or is it an orange in the presence of an apple? Suppose that in the past the company didn't have the same global presence. Suppose that its reputation had suffered a blow, and it was more difficult to recruit back then. Suppose that there was a shortage of expertise in the hiring pool? All of those issues would have a bearing on whether the comparison is relevant or not. And that's not all. What if other companies of similar size and international presence pay far more, or less, and always have?

When someone offers a comparison, if it isn't clear that the comparison is relevant, stop the conversation and ask. Do a quick check to see whether everyone is on the same page about the context of the situation and about how the comparison being raised will help you get your work done. Don't fear a blunt approach: Ask, "Is that relevant to what we're discussing?" and then ask, "How so?"

Who Is That in the Mirror?

Spotting sabotage when others commit it is difficult, but spotting sabotage when *you* are the saboteur is even harder.

It's almost impossible to spot Sabotage by Irrelevant Issues when the saboteur is looking at you in the mirror. It's like having a sign taped to your back— you can't read it. It's unlikely that after you wrap up an executive management meeting your senior vice president of marketing will clap you on the back and say: "Lousy meeting, Bill. You really can't stay on topic for more than twenty seconds, can you?"[1]

So how can you tell when you are an Irrelevant Issues Saboteur?

Get yourself a truth-teller. A consigliere. Someone who can offer direct, honest advice at critical points. Only occasionally will this person come from inside the organization, because your truth-teller's position and well-being can't be affected by you in any significant way. For one senior leader at a professional services practice, the truth-teller was the office administrative manager at headquarters. She had been with the firm for a long time; she was nearing retirement; she didn't have any alliances; she had learned over the years the art of keeping a confidence; and she had watched most of the partners "grow up" from the time they joined as wet-behind-the-ears associates. This person didn't ask her to be his truth-teller; she had taken the job upon herself, offering him pointed, honest advice at critical points in his career.

Who could yours be? He or she should not be someone in your family or someone who reports directly to you. You can ask anyone who is outside your group, though—anyone who has had significant experience in the area. If you are in a more informal working group, you could tap someone with a good reputation who is close to retirement, or who held your job in the past and is no longer gunning for a promotion. If you work at a high level in a large organization, you might consider engaging your outside counsel. Tell that person that you need him or her to do more than communicate with you through innuendo; you need him or her to be explicit.

Clearly the truth-teller won't be at all of your meetings. But this person will know your habits. You may not like everything you hear from your truth-teller, but you should listen anyway. It's like having a personal trainer. Or eating more fiber. Maybe you won't like the process, but the results are important.

Who Would Have Thought?

The OSS team members responsible for writing the original *Simple Sabotage Field Manual* clearly spent time dissecting the workings of organizations, drilling down layer by layer to identify vulnerable spots. Maybe they looked in their mirrors, too, to uncover personal weaknesses that could infect and spread through other organizations. Who would have thought that something as innocent as a simple digression could be so disruptive to a working group?

All of the sabotage tactics that they identified seem innocent on their face. For instance, who would have thought that haggling over the precise wordings of communications could rise from being an annoying habit to the level of deliberate, devastating sabotage. And yet it does, as we demonstrate in the next chapter.

5

Sabotage by Haggling

Haggle over precise wordings
of communications,
minutes, resolutions.

It's unlikely that the authors of the *Simple Sabotage Field Manual* haggled over every word in that brief but powerful pamphlet—discussing whether the word "communications" was too vague and the word "memos" would work better. They couldn't afford to delay publication simply because they were debating the wording of the sabotage tactics they presented. They had a war to fight and win. There was no time to waste.

They were hoping, however, that their enemies *would* waste plenty of time by deliberately haggling over every word. They knew that even small time-wasters can add up to a significant loss of time and energy. Fast-forward to seventy years later and the very act of sabotage they were encouraging is costing working groups hours and hours of lost productivity.

In the interest of making messages as effective as possible, it's easy to commit Sabotage by Haggling without realizing it. It's important to take care with words. In order to survive in today's digital world, we need to communicate constantly and quickly with colleagues, employees, customers, donors, partners, analysts, and shareholders through a myriad of channels. And one small error in wording that allows for misinterpretation can go viral in minutes and cause lasting damage to the people or organizations that put it out there. (More than 100 trillion emails, 8.6 trillion text messages, and 200 billion tweets go out annually; with that volume, it's likely that people misinterpret others' words pretty often.)

When people quibble about the wording of these communications—social media messages, mission statements, policies, press releases, meeting minutes, or resolutions—significant angst, frustration, resentment, and scheduling delays can occur. If ever there was a situation where the saying "Don't let the perfect become the enemy of the good" fits, this is it.

Take the case of Erin, who sits down with a group of colleagues, passes out copies of a draft memo that she has written, and asks for feedback. She has already spent most of a day working on this draft, and she's happy with the result. It has been a labor of love, after all. This memo invites members of her church community to the annual fund-raising auction event, highlighting some of the auction items and other activities planned for the evening, describing how important the auction has been in the past, and asking for volunteers.

But Erin is taken aback by the response. No one is pleased with the memo. At one point in the discussion, a surprisingly high-volume argument erupts over whether the words "not only" have to be followed somewhere by the words "but also." ("Why 'also'?" Erin asks. "Because that's the way it should be," is the emphatic answer from one of the other attendees.) An hour later, everyone is exhausted. What's worse, the memo is in complete disarray.

As people file out of the room, they hand Erin their copies of the memo, covered with crossed-out words, exclamation points, and tiny cramped writing in the margins. Everyone is grumpy and the meeting is deemed a disaster by all. Even worse, it looks like the committee chair, Mark, might resign from the planning group. This meeting, he muttered darkly as he left, pushed him over the edge. How had that happened? Was it really because Valerie had argued with Mark over the words "going forward"? Who cared about whether the words "going forward" or "in the future" were better? Was there any real difference?

Erin was supposed to send this memo out tomorrow; now it wouldn't be ready.

Well-intended actions. Yes. But sabotage? Absolutely.

What started as a session intended to improve the quality of a memo degenerated quickly into bad feelings and counterproductive actions. The members of this group are heading off to the next part of their day in bad moods. They're going to be distracted. The frustration they feel with Erin and her memo may translate into frustration with the next people they meet, even if those people have nothing to do with the memo. They're also going to feel pressure: Erin because she is now behind schedule, and the others because they've also lost time, are irritated, and feel as if they've failed at something.

Now picture another scenario: Erin emails the memo to everyone for review. They mark it up privately and get it back to her with their feedback. She is still overwhelmed when she sees the number of marks on her work and spends time accepting and rejecting the various suggestions. But she has to admit that the process is helpful.

Claire spotted several grammatical errors. Mark prevented her from sounding arrogant. Paola's turn of phrase in the last paragraph made her sound witty. She also added some important content (among other suggestions that Erin chose not to take). The revised memo is better because of the group effort: shorter, more to the point, even compelling.

In this case, Erin is *not* a victim of Sabotage by Haggling. She sends out the revised memo to the group, with a note thanking them all and explaining some of her reasons for accepting and rejecting suggestions. She asks them to read through this document but cautions that they are past the major revision stage. If they spot an error, they ought to respond; otherwise, it's going out. Time is of the essence.

Two colleagues respond immediately, saying, "Looks good to go." The others get back to her by the next morning with a variety of small changes, some of which she incorporates. She's happy with the finished product and grateful to the members of the committee.

The individuals in this group had the same reactions to the communication in both scenarios. But in one, they were Haggling Saboteurs. In the other, Erin's approach neatly sidestepped the trap.

Spotting the Haggle

Hagglers can perform a valuable and necessary service. They can push people to think, encourage them to consider more powerful words or ideas, and potentially help create a higher quality product—in some cases, they can even avert a potential embarrassment or disaster. They become unintentional Haggling Saboteurs only when they're left unchecked, and they draw the people they're with into an editing exercise that has no end in sight. The experience can deflate an otherwise enthusiastic effort, cause delays in the timeline, and make everyone present (and those waiting for the final product) frustrated and resentful.

That's why it's important to recognize Haggling Saboteurs up front. Let's look at three major types.

The Defender

The most common and passionate haggler is the Defender. This person's focus can be anything—a word, a phrase, the overall message, the tone.

Like any self-respecting cat that wants to mark its territory, Defenders can't resist the urge to mark a document—the email announcement, the meeting minutes, the press release, the client proposal. But that's usually okay. Defenders can provide a valuable service to the team if they are challenging the group to set the quality standard higher than it was before, test the quality of the message, and identify weaknesses in its structure.

Defenders become Haggling Saboteurs, however, when they refuse to relinquish their perspective on the document even when it's clear that the group disagrees or is ready to move to another topic. The Defender is thinking: "If I can just make the point one more time, maybe I can find one person to take my side, to be my ally. And once that happens the group will definitely see it my way and will make the change."

(Defenders, by the way, can be deliberate, purposeful saboteurs if, at bottom, they disagree with whatever *decision* has led to the creation of the document at hand; since they can't do anything about that, they attack the document itself.)

The Wordsmith

Wordsmiths want to change the document primarily to improve clarity and style; often, they're very valuable. Take, for example, the following sentence, which used to appear on the Federal Aviation Administration's website about the agency's program to reduce the number of collisions between birds and airplanes: "Over $300 million annually is lost due to wildlife strikes in the United States alone."

What does the sentence mean, really? Is it talking about just bird strikes even though it says "wildlife strikes"? Is the cost just about physical damage to property, or does it include the cost of flights delayed or diverted? A Wordsmith would most likely see this potential for misinterpretation and suggest a clearer sentence. In fact, one probably did, given that the sentence isn't on the website anymore.

Wordsmiths start out innocently with a couple of suggestions to rephrase a sentence or two: "I really don't like the way we've worded that phrase. Perhaps we could change X to Y, or A to B." But when their questions regarding the wording continue with great frequency and long after the group has decided that moving on to other topics would be more productive, then Wordsmiths have become Haggling Saboteurs.

Consider your typical session to develop an organization's mission statement. It starts out with great energy and enthusiasm as ideas fly around the room. However, all that soon dissipates as the Wordsmiths emerge and long discussions ensue around different words or phrases in the mission: "Do we 'serve' our customers, or are we 'responsive' to them?" "Is it 'transformational' or 'evolutionary'?" As discussions get longer, frustration increases, and the group wonders whether the wordsmithing is adding any value to the process.

The Grammar Police

Grammar Police go from one sentence to another pointing out every single grammatical, spelling and punctuation error. They start at sentence one and go from there. The lens they use does not include anything related to the *substance* of the communication.

Their comments focus on crucifying what they perceive to be incorrect grammar. They attempt to make sure that every sentence is constructed perfectly on the basis of their understanding of the rules of syntax and language. And they don't just correct what they perceive to be grammatical errors—they make sure that everyone else understands the precise grammatical rule that's been broken.

The Grammar Police sound like this:

> "In the first sentence, you need a comma. You should always use a comma before the word 'and' in a list."

> "In the second sentence of the third paragraph, you're using a double negative."

> "In the last paragraph on page three, the sentence where you say 'my wife and I' should say 'my wife and me.'"

> "In the fourth sentence of the second paragraph on page three, you split an infinitive."

Undoubtedly, appropriate use of grammar and punctuation is critical to effective communication. Quality proofreading is a necessity. In fact, if the Grammar Police know what they're talking about and have a solid track record, they can save writers and organizations from embarrassment.

When do the Grammar Police cross the line and commit Sabotage by Haggling? When, after the first two or three edits, it is apparent that a long list will follow, and the suggestions they are bringing to the table involve grammar and punctuation and nothing else. And although every comment may be of equal weight in the eyes of the Grammar Police, they don't try to prioritize the changes or offer to provide the suggestions in a different forum. They do, however, make sure that everyone understands the rationale for each change. It's not long before eyes start to glaze over, and the energy is sucked out of the room.

The Defender, the Wordsmith, and the Grammar Police are the Haggling Saboteurs we commonly see at work—we're sure there are others. In fact, it's not uncommon to encounter several of these saboteurs in the room at once. We've seen situations where several Wordsmiths went back and forth constantly massaging and refining every sentence of a document, memo, or proposal.

What's more troubling? These Haggling Saboteurs are often encouraged—by us.

Don't Encourage
Sabotage by Haggling

More often than not, the people seeking feedback are the ones who encourage Sabotage by Haggling. They tend to do two things wrong: They ask the wrong question, and they don't provide a clear path to closure.

The Wrong Question

Too often, managers ask for feedback on a piece of communication by simply asking, "What feedback do you have?" This question, though short and sweet, is a clear invitation for anyone, in particular Haggling Saboteurs, to offer and debate suggestions that are general and unfocused—or in some cases, even specific, but in areas that are not the most critical to discuss.

Take the case of Maura, the head of marketing for a consumer products company, looking for input on the email she is going to send as part of a marketing campaign for a new product. She innocently asks a group of her colleagues in a meeting, "What feedback do you have on the latest draft of the product launch email to our customers?" Maura might as well have thrown a piece of red meat to a pack of wolves.

The feedback comes fast and furious from various angles and altitudes.

John, a certified member of the Grammar Police offers: "You're mixing verb tenses throughout; just pick one and go with it."

Barry, a Wordsmith, has five suggested modifications, each involving something along the lines of taking the second part of a sentence and making it the first.

Jill, a Defender, presents more substantive word changes, which Maura rejects one by one on the grounds that they are changing the meaning of the offer. Twenty minutes later, Jill is still vigorously pushing her ideas and Maura has to insist that the group move on. "Jill, we're talking about the email, not the idea," she snaps, and Jill finally retreats, fuming.

But others aren't dissuaded, and sixty minutes later an exhausted Maura, now armed with piles of feedback, adjourns the meeting with the realization that she never received feedback on the part of the marketing campaign she and the team were hoping to receive—whether or not the email is enticing enough to get 20 percent of their customers to try the new product. If only she had asked a more targeted question, along the lines of "Imagine you are one of our customers. Would this email entice you to try the new product? If not, what specifically should we change in the email to increase the probability that it would?"

No Clear Path to Closure

When there is disagreement in the feedback process, a clearly defined path of closure is needed. Generally, feedback from a group on communication pieces falls into two categories: points of view held by all or the majority of the people in the room, and points of view held by people who do not agree. The first category of feedback is easy to handle because consensus is typically easier to obtain. It's the feedback that falls into the second category that the group debates ad nauseam. And as the haggling persists, the level of frustration among the participants increases as it becomes clearer that establishing consensus will not be possible. Worse yet, in the absence of a clear agreement on how the final decision will be made (the closure mechanism), the tension in the room is heightened further.

Consider Blake, the head of strategy at a large investment company, who needs closure on the company's latest strategy map—a one-page visual that depicts the organization's mission, vision, and key strategic priorities for the next three years.

Blake and his team had conducted several sessions to develop the strategy, drawing on input from thirty senior executives and other stakeholders. Now he stands in front of those thirty executives. He needs to make sure he has this group's support before it goes to the board in a week. He poses the question: "Is there anything on this map that you think we should change?"

Several hands shoot into the air. Blake diligently considers every suggested change. Some are relatively minor and consistent with each other. Others, however, are substantive and conflicting. Wordsmiths and Defenders are out in force, and as hard as Blake tries, he can't get them to agree.

The clock is ticking and the pressure is mounting. Blake is in trouble. Why are they so eager to discuss this? he wonders. He thought he had given them plenty of opportunity for input early in the process, but apparently it had not been enough. What can he do now to reach a consensus and make the board deadline? Is it even possible?

Of course, Blake should have scheduled this meeting sooner than one week before the board meeting, and then there's the question of why his team's earlier efforts to collect input weren't sufficient. The real issue, however, is the lack of a clear path to closure. In other words, who is going to make a decision when the group appears to be at an impasse? The CEO? Blake himself? Or will the majority rule and a vote be taken? None of this was clear to Blake or the group as the haggling continued with no end in sight and no clearly understood process in place to resolve it.

Stop the Haggle

Once you spot Haggling Saboteurs at work, it's important to stop them before the constant quibbling produces frustration and resentment, which at worst could be directed at you. This is especially true if you're the person who drafted the communication and find yourself standing in front of a room of people trying to gather feedback or reach closure, like Blake (even if you're the person who allowed the haggling to get destructive in the first place). Here are two ways you can deal with Sabotage by Haggling in the moment.

Raise the Bar

As soon as you become aware that some people have crossed the line from providing helpful feedback to becoming Haggling Saboteurs, stop the conversation and ask the group to give you their major points of feedback—those critical few items that at this stage are really causing individuals heartburn as they review the material.

Jen, head of HR at a retail chain, did just that when the level of quibbling during a session to approve a new corporate policy was beginning to suck the energy from the room. Jen told the group:

I really appreciate your feedback, but I'm
not sure the document is ready for this
sort of scrutiny. At the risk of cutting the
conversation short, I'd like to ask each of you
to write down your three or four major points
of feedback on the draft, write your name
on the page, and hand them to me. And by
"major" I mean the points that you consider
to be "must haves," areas that if the memo goes
out with this wording, there is a possibility
we'll regret it later. What language is in here
that might represent a potential "land mine"?

Fifteen minutes later Jen had eight pages—one
from each attendee—each with a few points of substantive feedback that represented the "must have"
changes to the policy. Over the next three days, Jen
reviewed the suggestions, incorporated some of them
in the document, asked additional questions, identified areas where she received conflicting feedback,
and followed up directly with individuals to explain
her rationale for not including some of their suggestions. Nice save, Jen.

Reframe the Conversation

Another way to deal with Haggling Saboteurs is to
reframe the conversation by tightening the focus
of the feedback you are asking for. Reframing the

conversation in this way can be very effective in producing feedback from the group in the areas where you know you need it.

Brian, the head of development at a private school, needed input from members of the school's Development Committee on a draft of a letter to the school community that outlined the latest capital campaign. The letter would launch a campaign to raise $5 million over three years to cover numerous facility upgrades. This was far more money than the school had ever raised in its one-hundred-year history. The campaign would also include phone calls, social media, and a series of events. Brian's team had spent hours putting the campaign together, and the letter would set the tone for the rest of the campaign.

Brian began to walk through the letter with the committee. The haggling started almost immediately. One committee member didn't like the way a sentence was worded in the opening paragraph. A second disagreed. A third thought the closing could be more powerful. And on and on it went for thirty minutes. Brian could feel the tension rising in the room. So he decided to reframe the conversation toward what he really needed from the group and told them:

> This is terrific feedback, all of which we've
> noted. But in our remaining thirty minutes,
> let's hear your thoughts on the overall tone

of the letter, which will affect the tone of the whole campaign. Is it too aggressive? Not aggressive enough? Just right? This is a big raise for the school. We've never done anything like this before. And your feedback on this particular point would be extremely valuable.

Immediately, the conversation became more focused, and Brian began to receive the type of feedback he needed. He knew his team could tighten the language used in the letter, which was ultimately his decision anyway. But he needed to hear the committee's views on how aggressive they wanted him and his team to be. He realized he should have asked this question at the onset, but at least he was able in the end to steer the discussion to get what he needed.

Avoid the Haggle

To minimize the possibility of encountering Sabotage by Haggling, you need to spend time crafting and refining your approach to developing your communication piece, specifically with an eye toward the feedback you need along the way. Don't shortchange this. We often see the same talented managers who possess laserlike focus on writing the piece—with careful consideration of the audience, the key messages, the structure—treat the process of gathering feedback from key individuals as an afterthought.

Higher quality communications result from allowing others to provide input and crafting forums for substantive points to be debated productively along the way. But without the right approach, the potential for Haggling Saboteurs to emerge increases significantly. Being intentional and thoughtful about how feedback will be provided and creating forums for discussions to occur are critical to immunizing yourself from the Haggling Saboteur. Some steps for you to consider follow.

Of course, not all communications are created equal. Some may require review by four people; others may need to go to a broad swath of employees for input; others may need to go to the legal team for review. You can dial these steps up or down as needed.

Make a Plan

Before you begin the effort to craft your communication piece—whether it be a press release or an important customer letter—take the time to make a plan. In your plan, be sure to clearly define the process you will use to develop, review, and approve the communication. What are the key steps? Who should be involved? What are the roles and responsibilities of each person? What forums will be created to review the material? What's the timeline?

Share the plan with the key stakeholders early in the process so they can ask questions or suggest changes. Your plan doesn't have to be complicated and should serve to set expectations so people understand the process and when they can provide input along the way.

Consider Who Needs to Be Involved

As you develop your communication pieces, think carefully about who needs to weigh in and when. In some cases, you might need feedback from a large group, while others may need only a few folks to contribute. Often, early in the process of developing a communication piece, the input you need may require lots of ideas and some creative thinking. A larger group—from ten to twenty—is preferable if your goal is to gather as many ideas as possible. For example, the head of marketing at an insurance company who had recently launched an effort to revamp his company's website gathered twenty individuals from across the organization for a day to solicit feedback and ideas. Table discussions and breakout groups were held to solicit a range of perspectives on everything from the website's intended audience, key messages, structure, and potential content. No decisions were made, but a lot of ideas were generated.

If you are farther along in the process and are seeking input on an existing draft of a memo, proposal, or even a website—or perhaps exploring various options that you might pursue—a relatively smaller group of six to twelve participants is preferred. We often see rooms packed unnecessarily, which is counterproductive. Limit invitations for these sessions to key stakeholders; don't invite every team member who could possibly attend.

If you are at a point where a decision is needed on a communication piece, it is best to limit the session to key decision makers. Keep in mind that you might need a decision made at various points, not just at the end. Experience suggests an inverse relationship between the number of people involved and the ability to make a decision, so when a decision is required, do your best to keep the group somewhere between three to six participants.

Be Specific About the Feedback You Want

As we saw with Maura, asking the simple question, "What feedback do you have?" tends to invite a wide range of comments and certainly does not guarantee you will receive the feedback you need. And it is fertile ground for Haggling Saboteurs—all the Defenders, Grammar Police, and Wordsmiths—to emerge and waste valuable time haggling. Set the boundaries. Be specific about the feedback you are looking for and, just as important, the feedback you don't want. If you want input on a specific aspect of the communication, ask for it. And if you don't want feedback on something, take it off the table or find a way for individuals to provide input at another time.

Circulate in Advance the Material That Needs Feedback

When most people show up for a meeting designed to gather feedback, they are handed a document for the first time when they arrive, asked to take a few minutes to review it, and then asked what they think. This causes two problems: First, the quality of the feedback is not as high as it could be, given the short period of time individuals are given to reflect on the document. Second, the chances are higher of individuals realizing an important point of feedback *after* the meeting that they should have offered *during* the meeting—which of course means they will take the next opportunity to add their two cents on the matter, regardless of whether it's the right time to do so.

To avoid this trap, send your draft memos, policies, or proposals to individuals before the deadline with a reasonable lead time.

If a meeting will occur to discuss what you sent, tell the participants in your cover note that you are assuming they will read the material in advance so "we can spend our time during the meeting discussing your input versus presenting the material." Include specific instructions outlining what individuals should consider as they read the material before the meeting, and how they should provide the feedback.

These instructions can be relatively simple. For example, one of our clients recently sent out a copy of a strategy document one week before a critical review meeting. He asked participants to consider one major question: "Do you think if we follow the strategy as described that we will achieve our stated goal of doubling the size of our business in three years? Please bring any questions or concerns to the meeting."

Another client looking for a thorough and meticulous line-by-line review of a memo to go to the board of directors sent the draft memo to a group of five and asked them to submit their suggested modifications in tone, style, and grammar electronically. She gave them three days to send their comments and sent a reminder one day before the deadline.

In both cases, because participants received the material in advance and had several days to respond, the quality of the feedback and the discussion (in the case of the meeting) was heightened significantly and the Haggling Saboteurs were kept at bay.

Find Some Trusted Reviewers

Find a few individuals you trust who can review your communications before they go to a broader audience. These individuals should proofread the material, which of course could save you from potential embarrassment and keep the Grammar Police at bay. Most importantly, they should be able to put themselves in the shoes of the intended audience and provide candid feedback if part or all of the material misses the mark.

Be Clear Who Has the Final Call

Make sure there is complete clarity over who will decide what is ultimately distributed, published, and communicated. There's a reason that newspapers have editors responsible for each department, front-page editors, op-ed page editors, and editors in chief. It's clear where the buck stops. Endless haggling can often be avoided when everyone understands who has the final call. Debates can occur and different points of view can be put forward, but when all is said and done, one individual should have approval authority, and everyone should know who that person is.

Forewarned Is Forearmed

One of our clients once said, "We all learned about Maslow's hierarchy of needs—self-actualization, esteem, love/belonging, safety, and physiological.

Nobody ever talks about the sixth, hidden level: the need to edit other people's writing." Haggling over communications is natural; we're hardwired to do it. Unfortunately, we're also hardwired to do too much of it. When you see Sabotage by Haggling happening, take action to stop it before the Haggling Saboteurs create angst and resentment among the group. Better yet, take steps to prevent it from happening in the first place.

6

Sabotage by Reopening Decisions

Refer back to matters decided upon
at the last meeting and attempt
to reopen the question of the
advisability of that decision.

hen someone tries to reopen a decision, your
initial reaction probably isn't that you're being
sabotaged. It's more likely to be frustration—
"Seriously? You want to go over this again? I thought
it was settled! I would rather stick pins in my eyes
than go back and rehash this decision!"—followed by

a resigned response: "I'd better listen; this might be important."

The problem is that in a lot of cases, the ensuing conversation frequently does result in reopening the decision—and too often, the reasons for reopening the decision aren't as sound as they might seem in the moment. Passion (theirs), lack of confidence (maybe yours), and time pressure (everyone's) often cloud your judgment. And when that happens—and if it happens frequently—you're dealing with sabotage that has both short- and long-term consequences. That's probably why Sabotage by Reopening Decisions made the cut in the original OSS *Manual;* the "hurt them now, hurt them even more later" potential is great.

The Consequences of Sabotage by Reopening Decisions

In the immediate term, reopening a decision can cause resentment and confusion. For example, if a decision is reopened and those who made or were part of making the original decision are not consulted, they're probably going to be unhappy that their decision has been overruled behind their backs. They may try to sabotage the new decision—and this won't be inadvertent sabotage; it will be deliberate and direct.

What's more, people who moved ahead on the basis of what the original decision or game plan *was* now run the risk of losing time and focus as they re-orient themselves to (maybe) move in a different direction. People who were told to do something on the basis of the first decision now also have to be reined in—to stop what they're doing and even retract some of their work. Maybe they've already placed orders, reached out to clients or vendors, or put other plans in motion. How will they backtrack cleanly? It's not easy; loose ends can appear and multiply fast.

Reopening a decision can also lead to paralysis. Every activity that was supposed to happen (other plans that were supposed to be made, other issues that were supposed to be discussed) as a result of executing the first decision now has to stop while people are rethinking it and potentially changing course. What if other folks are waiting on the issues that were supposed to be decided on "today"? A lot can get out of sync fast when someone says, "I think we need to rethink this thing."

Say that you're building a house, and you're pretty far along in the construction process. Plumbing is done; electrical is roughed in. The contractor tells you he's going to work on the kitchen for the next few days. Two days later, your partner says he really would prefer that the stairs from the kitchen to the second floor be located on the other side of the sink. So you go to the contractor and say you're going to rethink the stairs, and you'll get back to him.

Now the contractor is frustrated: He has to stop work on the kitchen until you and your partner make a final decision. He has to alert the vendor who was providing the material for the stairs—changing the location might mean adjustments to the amount of material they need. The electrician also has to be on standby as it's likely that a wall will have to be re-opened. Everyone is frustrated and waiting in limbo. If you do decide to move the stairs, do you think the process will be smooth, efficient, and cost-effective? Yeah, sure it will.

The long-term consequences of reopening decisions are even more daunting. If someone in your organization reopens decisions frequently, and it's easy for him or her to do so, then other people will follow suit. Eventually, you'll have two bad cultural habits on your hands. First, over time, people will become increasingly hesitant to *make* firm decisions—even small ones—in the first place. Why bother when they can be overruled so quickly? Second, once decisions are made, people will think twice before *acting* on them for fear (or expectation) that somewhere down the line, they will be told to stop, reverse, and go in a different direction. (Or they'll just ignore decisions entirely, especially if they don't agree with them.)

We've seen this happen in towns where school boards, council members, and town employees gain a reputation for inaction. We've seen it in organizations where employees don't jump on projects right away because of the high probability that the decision to start the project at all will be changed. We've seen it at very personal levels where someone rethinks going to college or graduate school or relocating to a new city or pursuing a particular career and becomes increasingly dissatisfied and uncertain while going over the same ground again and again.

It doesn't have to be that way. And yet, we fall prey to Sabotage by Reopening Decisions all the time. Like the other forms of sabotage in this book—and remember, the original *Simple Sabotage Field Manual* was written by some of the smartest spymasters of the time—this kind of sabotage isn't easy to recognize. That's because many times, reopening a decision is a good thing.

To Reopen or to Stay the Course and Damn the Torpedoes?

That's right. It's not always a bad thing to reconsider a decision and even reverse course. Doing so can signal a healthy relationship, or work environment, where people aren't afraid to speak up. Doing so can signal a vested interest in doing what's best for the cause, the organization, or the team. Doing so can save brands and businesses.

Consider PepsiCo's 2009 experience with its Tropicana brand. The company spent roughly $30 million on a new look for its juice design (a photo of juice in a glass). Almost instantly, sales suffered and customers complained that the design looked "generic" or like a "discount store brand." A mere seven weeks after the new design's launch, PepsiCo scrapped it and returned to the original look (an orange with a straw in it). It may have been tough for the people at PepsiCo to reopen that decision and kiss its investment goodbye, but it was the right move.

Reopening decisions can also prevent injury, or maybe even save lives. Consider a summer camp whose diving platform has been struck by lightning just days before the camp is supposed to host other camps at the Camp Pond Olympics. The camp director, together with the directors from the other camps, has been planning the event for months, but when she sees that the diving platform has been damaged, she asks the others to reconsider either the timing of the event or the location. Is the camp director a Reopening Decisions Saboteur? Of course not, because the situation had changed and a different set of relevant facts was available.

So how can you tell the difference between righteous "rethinking" and its flip side? By figuring out whether the person asking for the "do-over" has a justifiable reason for reopening the decision and, if so, weighing that reason against the risk of moving forward with the decision. The trick lies in being able to identify the reasons why people ask to reopen decisions. Understanding the motivation behind someone's request to reconsider a decision will help you determine when to cry, "Damn the torpedoes, full speed ahead!" or when to say, "You've got a point there; let's reconsider."

Our list of the six most common reasons people ask for decisions to be reopened follows.

"I've Been Wronged"

People sometimes try to reopen decisions simply because they feel that things should have gone their way the first time. When is this Sabotage by Reopening Decisions? When the reason for trying to backtrack is simply that the person asking to reopen the decision didn't like losing. These people, given the floor, will rehash the same arguments they made at earlier meetings, maybe in a louder voice, with a tinge of a whine.

We saw this situation recently at a meeting of twelve board members of a private high school. At a prior meeting, the board voted to make an offer on an $8 million building to expand the school to another location. Ten people had voted for making the offer; two had voted against it. The board had debated the offer and the property at length during two previous meetings. Well before the vote, a real estate broker had been called in to make sure that the school was offering a market price. The Finance Committee had analyzed the budget to make sure that the school could afford to buy, update, and maintain the property. The school's lawyers had signed off on the deal as well. Every board member had toured the property and been offered numerous opportunities to ask questions.

This meeting was supposed to be about the status of the offer and the hoped-for next step—renovation plans. But ten minutes into the meeting, Jane, one of the two directors who had voted "no," interjected: "As we discussed last time, I really think this is the wrong decision for the organization. I think we need to go in a different direction." Jane didn't like losing the first time around, but when asked for more detail, she recited almost verbatim the same arguments she had made previously. After a sixty-minute back and forth with other board members covering the same ground, the conversation produced the same outcome: stay the course.

Now, Jane could have given details that may have made a legitimate case for considering a new direction, such as "I just learned that the original building we tried to buy is coming back on the market," or "I know of another building that is going to come on the market in the same area that's in better shape and configured better for our needs." But she didn't. She just hit "replay" on all of her old arguments.

How could the committee chair have cut her off at the pass? By asking, at the first sign of her objection, "Jane, do you have any new and relevant information to bring to the table?—something we didn't already know about before this?"

That's the best way to stop the Reopening Decisions Saboteur in his or her tracks. Ask, "What's changed since we made our decision?" If nothing has, then there's no reason to move backwards.

"I'm Biased!" (I Just Don't Know It)

Most decisions—especially those in fast-moving industries, startups, or small groups where comprehensive "research" is a luxury—are made without the benefit of perfect or complete information. Sometimes it works out, but sometimes it doesn't. So when someone bursts into the room and says, "Stop everything! Hit reverse!" we're primed to think we ought to pay close attention—the person might have the missing information needed to make a "perfect" decision.

The problem is, a lot of times that person has a bias that we don't know about—and that he or she probably doesn't know about either. And so that person's perception of the situation isn't objective.

For example, organizations of all shapes and sizes are always looking for ways to free resources to fund new growth initiatives. One way to do that is to stop something that the organization is currently doing and divert those resources to the new growth areas. Time and again, we've watched people who are great at developing and starting new programs almost do a Jekyll-and-Hyde transformation when it comes to sticking to their decisions to *stop* doing something. They reopen those decisions . . . and make them again. Then, just before it's time to pull the plug for the second, third, or even fourth time, they say "Wait! What about *X* or *Y*?"

What's going on? Why are these otherwise stellar individuals morphing into saboteurs? Because each project, or line of business, has an owner somewhere who believes in it strongly and is emotionally invested in its success. And when asked to stop even the most obvious programs, those owners just cannot bring themselves to let go. Behind the scenes, after the "stop" decision has been made and they have agreed to it, they seek out information that seems to confirm their position while ignoring information against it.

It's impossible to take biases out of decision-making, but it's good to be aware of the influence they can have. Often, when people with biases try to reopen a decision, they will appeal to others' emotions to get them on board. Either that, or they will bring information to the table that seems new and relevant (to them) but truly is not.

That's where you can call to the fore the lessons you learned regarding Sabotage by Irrelevant Issues (see Chapter 4). Acknowledge the person's concern, but put the objection in a parking lot for consideration at a later time, either at the end of the meeting, or later on. You might say, "I understand what you're saying. It's clear you have lots of passion about it." Doing this will let the person know that his or her opinion matters, but at the moment, it's not going to be helpful to the group to focus on it. But if you put something in the parking lot, make sure you follow up with that person—soon—to hear the concerns in full and see whether the suggestion to reopen the decision is the right thing to do.

"We Were Rushed!"

When people want to reopen a decision on the grounds that it was made in haste, it's easy to think that they are trying to prevent the group from a "Ready! Fire! Aim!" situation. Good behavior? If it's clear that the decision-making process skipped a step, then yes.

The problem is, it's often too easy to buy into the idea that you've rushed into a decision, especially if the decision is about something big, say, involving significant amounts of money or a real change in direction. You may be lacking in confidence; you may fear the consequences if it turns out that you made the wrong call.

Consider Josh, the CIO of a company that owned and operated more than forty car dealerships. Josh was about to sign a contract on a software system that would help the company better manage its supply chain, which was fraught with all sorts of issues that resulted in numerous customer delays. The decision would easily run close to a million dollars. Josh and his team had had several meetings with each of their potential vendors, vetting them thoroughly and finally selecting one. Due diligence hadn't been easy, but Josh felt confident about the decision.

Then, just a day before he was to sign the contract, one of his direct reports, Sarah, came in with the news that a competing car business had signed with another vendor. The competitor was a strong one—a great company, smart owners—and Sarah suddenly doubted the research her own team had done.

Josh was worried. If Sarah was doubtful, shouldn't he be, too? Concerned that he was on the cusp of making a bad decision, he called an emergency meeting. "Should we do more homework?" he asked his team. "Sarah feels like we're rushing into the decision, and I'm inclined to agree. Let's take a little more time to evaluate the other vendors."

Two months later, after having reopened their decision, they still didn't have a contract with a vendor. Their original top-choice vendor, impatient and losing interest, was upping its price. Due to continuing supply chain issues, cars were not available so customers were taking their business elsewhere. What's more, word from the grapevine indicated that the system the competitor bought wasn't working out very well. So Josh felt pressure to sign with someone, anyone. And he knew he wasn't going to be able to take his time to implement the new software—wherever they got it—with the care that he should. His team was up against a wall.

Sarah was an innocent (under-confident) Reopening Decisions Saboteur, and Josh (fearing she was right) allowed himself to become her unwitting accomplice. Fear and under-confidence are powerful motivators. If you think either of these emotions is in the driver's seat, when someone pulls the "We were rushed!" card, ask for a fact-based answer to the question, "Let's assume we had more time to decide; what would we do with it that we haven't already done?" If there's no grounded answer, then you have a great argument for staying the course.

"You Didn't Ask Me"

Sometimes people might try to reopen a decision because they weren't involved in the decision-making process. Maybe they disagree with the decision; maybe not. But they weren't consulted, so their nose is out of joint. In an attempt to thwart the decision, they claim that the outcome won't be good—and the implication is that had they been consulted, the decision would have been different.

If someone asking to reopen a decision can't give solid details about why his or her input or perspective would lead to a different decision, then you're looking at a Reopening Decisions Saboteur.

Often such saboteurs aren't very hard to spot. They're the ones who think they know everything. We've encountered many of these "know-it-alls" in our careers. They believe that they're the go-to person. They tend to monopolize conversations, dismiss input from others, and have a "my way or the highway" attitude.

But sometimes, they are highly respected individuals—founders of organizations, or close to retirement and trying (unsuccessfully) to pass the torch and get out of the way. Maybe they were previous decision makers and are now in a supporting role. The trouble is, they are still on the stage, and when they speak, they steal the scene. And if they want to reopen a decision—even though they don't have the authority to do so—people do it.

To minimize the risk of this sort of situation, we suggest that you listen to Cyrus the Great, the Persian king who said, "Diversity in counsel, unity in command." In other words, make sure to get enough input from enough people before making a decision. Gathering input before a decision may seem like an obvious step, but managers often fail to take that step. Before making the call, the decision maker is wise to seek counsel from a broad range of people, including those who are likely to object and those who will carry out the decision once it's made. Hearing everyone out will increase the quality of the decision. But once the decision is made, it should stand.

We're not suggesting that you include anybody and everybody in the process, and we also know that the volume of input in and of itself doesn't guarantee a better outcome. But the more people you consult during the process, the stronger their support of the decision will be. Even if the decision does not go in their favor, they feel that you have considered and respected their opinions.

"I Didn't Tell You Before, but I'm Telling You Now"

When everyone seems to agree with a decision, but the room is quiet, take that as a warning. Arguably, whenever an individual in your group is asked for feedback, that person is expected to offer his or her thoughts candidly and directly. It's great when that happens. But here's the reality: It often doesn't happen, especially in a public setting (e.g., a large staff meeting in an organization, a general members meeting of an association, a community gathering) and especially if the decision is a high-stakes one.

We see this in meetings when employees of different levels are asked for feedback and the more junior people hesitate to offer a differing opinion in front of more senior people, especially their bosses. Instead, the usual suspects dominate the conversation and share their perspectives. The rest are silent, even if they don't agree. Sometimes, they know they won't "win," so they keep quiet and wait until after the decision is made to wage a behind-the-scenes campaign to sway support to their point of view. They don't want to cause a problem after the fact, but they don't see any other option. They don't feel as if they have a voice in the moment.

This can have a disastrous effect on a group of people who are trying to come to a decision together. Consider the times when senior leaders do broad-scale assessments of their key people in what are often called "calibration sessions," in which employees are assessed and ranked on the basis of their performance during the previous year. As Annie Drapeau, an operating partner at Bain Capital, told us: "People's futures can really hang in the balance here. The last thing you want to have happen is for people in the meeting to hold back and save their comments for a later time."

Suppose that indeed happens: Some people don't share all their impressions of a candidate at a calibration session, and someone is promoted on the strength of the few comments that *are* made. Then a few weeks later, it comes out that several people who provided input (or were supposed to) had withheld some critical reservations about the person being assessed. Maybe they *were* more junior level employees who didn't feel comfortable offering dissenting opinions in the face of positive reports from more senior employees. Now their views have come to light, but there's already a domino effect in the works. The promotion has been made; the newly "open" position is being advertised; interviews and other calibration sessions are taking place. As Drapeau put it, "Moving backwards is going to be incredibly difficult, even if it turns out that it's the right thing to do."

One tool we have used (and seen used) effectively to inoculate organizations from acts of sabotage related to individuals not expressing their opinions candidly and directly is to establish the following ground rule: *Qui tacet consentire videtur,* or "Silence denotes consent." This rule does a good job of getting people to open up, however reluctant (or passive aggressive) they may be feeling—or risk never having their points of view influence the decision at hand.

Here's how it works: If you are seeking input in anticipation of making a decision on an issue, provide a forum or mechanism for others to offer their input and to debate the various points of views. Depending on the organization and the scope of the decision, we recommend well-designed meetings, surveys, electronic polls, and other techniques to facilitate getting opinions and different points of view on the table (anonymously or otherwise). Before those whom you've invited to provide feedback present their input, let them know of the ground rule: Silence denotes consent. If you do not hear (or see, in some cases) any points of view that are different from the predominant position that has emerged, you will assume that everyone agrees with it. You can then proceed with greater confidence that the minority opinion has been heard.

"I Know We Agreed to Something, but I'm Going to Implement Something Different"

The last and probably the most insidious and damaging form of Sabotage by Reopening Decisions happens while implementing a decision *after* the decision makers' work is done. In the words of Noel Tichy and David Ulrich, "CEOs [and we would submit most managers] tend to overlook the lesson Moses learned several thousand years ago—namely, getting the ten commandments written down and communicated is the easy part; getting them implemented is the challenge."[1]

Consider the experience of a manager of a financial services company. He had been a member of a group involved in making a decision, but then, as he told us: "I knew what we agreed to at the meeting, but when I got back to my team and talked to them about it, they had some good thoughts to add. So, while we're going in the same direction that the group decided on, we took the liberty of making some changes in how we go about it."

He and his team had, in effect, reopened the decision on the sly—during execution. In fact, nobody else will find out that his team has altered the decision until it's discovered at some point down the road. Meanwhile, others are moving along as if they know what's going on. The repercussions could be enormous. And the more time that passes before discovery, the greater the divide between what was agreed upon originally and what has actually been executed.

To get out in front of this sort of situation, first, develop a communication plan for the decision—what should be communicated, in what form, by whom, and to whom—to avoid any confusion or misunderstanding about what was decided and why. Second, make sure you understand who is accountable for implementing the decision. This may be someone different from the person accountable for making the decision. And third, put periodic checkpoints in place to make sure the implementation of the decision is tracked and monitored—and is progressing in a way consistent with what was intended.

Don't Let Reopening Decisions Become a Habit

In any situation where a decision is questioned, you'll need to weigh the cost/benefit of reopening the decision against the cost/benefit of staying the course. In certain cases, it might make sense to reopen, especially if new and relevant information has become available. But here's the reality. If it's too easy to reopen decisions, then people in the organization will hesitate to make them. If decisions are not viewed as permanent and final, then people will think twice before implementing them, especially those who thought it was the "wrong decision" in the first place. If you decide with careful consideration, do a good job of collecting input from the right people, communicate your decisions clearly, and then put checkpoints in place to track the progress of implementation, you'll be able to confidently fend off Reopening Decisions Saboteurs who try to reopen the decisions on the basis of their personal agendas.

You can't prevent people from attempting Sabotage by Reopening Decisions. What you *can* do, in addition to understanding why this kind of sabotage happens and addressing it in the moment, is improve your decision-making processes. By doing that, you will close at least some of the windows that would-be Reopening Decisions Saboteurs would otherwise slip through.

7

Sabotage by Excessive Caution

Advocate "caution." Be "reasonable" and urge your fellow-conferees to be "reasonable" and avoid haste, which might result in embarrassments or difficulties later on.

In the musical *How to Succeed in Business without Really Trying*, there's a scene where J. Pierpont Finch, a new employee starting out in the mailroom, is talking with an older employee, Mr. Twimble, who is showing Finch a medal the company gave him. Here's the conversation:

Mr. Twimble: Last month I became a quarter-of-a-century man.

J. Pierpont Finch: Oh, that's beautiful, a quarter-of-a-century.

Mr. Twimble: Quarter-of-a-century.

J. Pierpont Finch: How long have you been in the mail room?

Mr. Twimble: Twenty-five years. It's not easy to get this medal. It takes a combination of skill, diplomacy, and bold caution.

Not that there's anything wrong with a steady job in the mailroom. But suppose that's not what you want. Are too many of us boldly cautious, like Mr. Twimble? Are we "careful" and "reasonable" to the point where we hold ourselves back?

If we are, we might be practicing Sabotage by Excessive Caution.

Caution is a strange thing. Most of the time, it's a solid, smart idea to be cautious, or careful, or reasonable. It makes sense to avoid haste and also to try to keep others from jumping into things too quickly. You've heard the sayings: "Haste makes waste"; "Marry in haste, repent at leisure"; "Don't put the cart before the horse." They all make sense. Hit "send" on that angry email you just wrote while your blood is boiling, and you might regret it. Jump into a project with your colleagues without figuring out the scope of the thing, and you might find yourself in over your head. Throw caution to the winds, and you're likely to run into a lot of trouble, fast.

But err on the side of too much caution, and you might find yourself in the back of the pack. Err on the side of too much care, or hesitation, and you might sabotage yourself or your group, despite your best intentions. Consider what happens to these people and groups when they "exercise caution":

- The high school basketball team is cautioned excessively about committing fouls. Players lose their appetite for playing aggressively and as a result lose game after game. Their concern about committing fouls distracts them from their purpose: scoring, and keeping the other team from scoring. They also forget to enjoy the game.

- The staff members of a human resources department recognize the need for the senior leaders of their organization to get away from their daily work to talk about what it would take to expand their business to a new city. They start to design a retreat for that purpose. But they become so worried that the retreat will be seen as "exclusive" by others in the organization that they end up creating a twice-yearly series of rather pointless retreats for everyone. Too much "reason" compels these human resources professionals to spend time and energy on a needless pursuit.

- Graham Spanier, who was president of Penn State for sixteen years, kept advocating caution when it came to addressing the accusations of child sexual abuse against assistant football coach Jerry Sandusky. He was reportedly afraid of the potential negative publicity these accusations would attract. Just four days after Sandusky was arrested in 2011, Spanier found himself ousted. A year later, he was charged with eight counts of criminal activity, including perjury, conspiring to cover up Sandusky's misconduct, and child endangerment. An excess of caution made a "wait and see" approach to resolving a terrible situation seem sensible when more decisive action was warranted.

Eventually, too much caution or reason becomes an organizational habit. It becomes a cultural mantra that whispers, "Every silver lining has a cloud." It primes people to see all ideas through a lens of potential disaster, no matter how they are introduced or promoted. It prevents people from taking action quickly, even when it's necessary; it slows everybody down. It kills creativity and makes people scared to do much of anything at all. A cautious mind-set that permeates an organization is an intentional Excessive Caution Saboteur's dream. And that's precisely why the OSS included this sabotage tactic in the original *Manual*. In today's working groups, when the Sabotage by Excessive Caution is inadvertent, it's no less a nightmare.

Spotting Sabotage by Excessive Caution

In order to stop or prevent caution from thwarting your organization's efforts, first you have to be able to differentiate between good caution and caution that crosses the line into sabotage. This means learning how to differentiate between a "threat" and a "risk." A *threat* may always be present, but how great is the *risk* of that threat becoming a reality?

Here are two tactics that should help you answer that question. When faced with caution that seems it could be Sabotage by Excessive Caution in disguise, ask for facts, and draw up a list of "pros" and "cons."

Ask for Facts

Excessive Caution Saboteurs lurk in the shadows; facts are your flashlight. So when someone says, "This looks like a case of Ready–Fire–Aim. We need to be reasonable. We need to slow down!" ask why he or she thinks that's the case.

If you don't get any facts, you're facing Sabotage by Excessive Caution. Often, a person's caution is based on an emotional reaction rather than on a measured assessment of the situation. Consider: You want to go camping in New Hampshire. Someone raises the possibility that bears might kill you while you sleep. What do you do? Ask yourself: What is the *threat*? The threat is bears. Is the threat *real*? Yes, it is. But what about the *risk*? Is the risk high? Well, the New Hampshire Fish and Game Department website tells you that the last time someone was killed by a black bear in New Hampshire was in 1748! And black bears are the only type of bears that live in New Hampshire. So the risk is low. Facts can help you tell whether Sabotage by Excessive Caution might be at work.

This tactic is, well, not rocket science. Not even close. But in our experience, not enough people practice it.

Draw Up a "Pros and Cons" List

Sometimes when you ask for facts, you'll get one or two, but not enough to have an "Aha!" moment where you can point a finger and say: "J'accuse! Saboteur be gone!" (or, if the caution is well placed: "You have

a good point there; let's consider this some more").
Maybe the Bear Worrier points out that about five
thousand bears live in New Hampshire. That's a
fact. The Bear Worrier can cite the New Hampshire
Fish and Game Department as a source. The Bear
Worrier has identified a threat. But is that enough?
Probably not.

If you get *some* facts, and you're not sure how they
stack up, create a list of "pros and cons" so you can
see all together the advantages and the perceived
disadvantages of continuing with the course of action that you have decided on—and so you can see
whether the potential saboteur is advocating that
you abort or delay out of excessive caution. In the
case of the bears, you would find that knowing the
number of bears in New Hampshire is insufficient.
It's data, and it's powerful, but by itself, it doesn't tell
you anything about camping safety. You would need
additional facts, such as where the bears are concen-
trated, whether there is a season when they are more
likely to be seen or aggressive. What does the number five thousand tell you about their habits around
humans? Nothing. Fill in that additional data.

Then go through each of the "cons" and spend
some time quantifying the *probability* that they
would come to pass. If possible, assign a percentage—is the bad ending 90 percent likely to happen?
Fifty percent likely? Ten percent?

With your list in hand, also ask the group to consider how moving cautiously will affect whether the decision is implemented and how successful it will be. Will slowing down lower the risk of something bad happening, or just postpone it? Will being cautious result in a missed opportunity?

Your list of the pros and cons of following cautious advice will help you gain perspective by encouraging the group to think with their heads as well as their hearts—or wherever it is that fear comes from. The emphasis here is on your cons list—on gaining insight on what's driving the call for caution. This advice is similar to what we told you about gathering facts when people ask to reopen a decision because they were "rushed" into making it in the first place (see Chapter 6). That's not a coincidence. A "get the facts" approach—an approach that requires an injection of objectivity—is a useful antidote to any form of sabotage that feeds on emotion and perceived pressure.

Sometimes, you're going to find that it's hard to figure out the probability of something bad happening. Sometimes, assigning a percentage isn't possible. When that's the case, try another approach: Categorize or color-code the risk of the bad ending—high-medium-low, or red-yellow-green.

To get deep into the belly of the beast on assessing risk, we talked with one of the world's foremost experts on the topic, Brent Walder. Brent is the chief actuary of Prudential Retirement. He and his organization are responsible for assessing and quantifying the risk that accompanies the management of the retirement funds of millions of Americans. He has a mandate to protect those funds; he also has a responsibility to help them grow. Risk is his job, and his organization takes an extraordinarily disciplined approach to quantifying it. Here's his advice:

> I would advocate starting any assessment of risk by defining what success should look like. You need to know what success is so that you can capture risk and evaluate it in the right context. You want to minimize risk, sure, but you have to remember that minimizing risk isn't your only criterion for succeeding. It also helps to bucket your risk in types. Are you talking about competitive risks? Resource risks? Risks we understand well, or not at all? Where on the path to success does this risk fit? Doing that can also help you keep things in perspective.

It may be comforting to realize that even the experts on risk continue to need and use deliberate methods to put it in perspective.

Turning Sabotage by Excessive Caution into an Advantage

In some cases, the best way to deal with Sabotage by Excessive Caution is to pretend that you don't spot it for the sabotage that it is, and appear to give in to it. This approach works best when you know the would-be saboteur, and you know that he or she is often overly cautious because of anxiety or underconfidence. Think of it this way: Picture a man catching a large, heavy ball. If he stands still with a stiff back and tries to catch it, he may get knocked over. But if he moves a little with the momentum of the ball—backing up a bit, bending his legs—then he can catch the ball without falling. This kind of approach—giving a little to accomplish your greater goal—is what we're talking about. You'll be accepting the cautionary words of the would-be Excessive Caution Saboteur, but not letting him or her control you.

To do this, borrow a lesson from improvisational theater called, "Yes, and." Tina Fey explains it in her book *Bossypants* in this way:

> If we're improvising and I say, "Freeze, I have
> a gun," and you say, "That's not a gun. It's your
> finger. You're pointing your finger at me,"

> our improvised scene has ground to a halt.
> But if I say, "Freeze, I have a gun!" and you
> say, "The gun I gave you for Christmas! You
> bastard!" then we have started a scene because
> we have AGREED that my finger is in fact a
> Christmas gun.[1]

"Yes, and" in the context of Sabotage by Excessive Caution means to acknowledge what the other person is saying, and go from there. Essentially, this approach turns an Excessive Caution Saboteur's usual knee-jerk response, "Yes, but," on its head. If you take a "Yes, and" approach, you will often be able to continue on your course as planned. You're reassuring your concerned colleague that you hear what he or she is saying. And you're getting on with the business of the day. Sometimes, you'll find that by using a "Yes, and" approach, not only will you thwart attempted sabotage, but also you'll gain an unexpected benefit.

For example, suppose you run a sporting goods store and you're considering adding stand-up paddleboards (SUPs) to your inventory because you live in a town with two good-sized lakes and a few smaller ponds with summer rental cottages around them. Your business partner is advocating caution: Even though it's clear this sport is taking off, he says it's too risky an idea. The sport hasn't been introduced in your area yet, and he fears the investment won't pay off. You ask for specifics and learn that one of your partner's objections to adding SUPs to the inventory is that the owner of the area's marine supply store—your closest competitor—has stocked them in the past with dismal results.

Although the fact that your competitor tried and failed to sell SUPs worries your partner—a worrier by nature—you think differently. You say, "*Yes*, it is troubling that our competitor carried SUPs and wasn't able to sell them, *and* we should learn from his mistakes." Agreeing with the Excessive Caution Saboteur's concerns allows you to turn those concerns on their head. Looking deeply into why your competitor failed—the source of your partner's concern—allows you to avoid your competitor's fate.

At dinner that evening, you decide to buy fifteen SUPs and offer them for rent. At the end of the season, you'll sell them as-is at a discount. After investigating the liability of renting SUPs, and confirming coverage, you test the waters by advertising the scheme and start taking bookings for the summer season. With a fair number of reservations in hand, you purchase the SUPs.

You've addressed your partner's concerns—and not only have you stopped his call for caution from sabotaging a potentially profitable idea, but also you have mitigated the risks of implementing this idea by learning from your competitor's experience.

Inoculating Your Workgroup Against Sabotage by Excessive Caution

Rob was running a workshop at a large chemical company whose leaders were trying to get their chemists to be more innovative. Going in, he didn't know that the organization's culture had succumbed to Sabotage by Excessive Caution. He found out what he was up against only when one of the chemists raised a hand about half an hour into the program. "I'm not sure you understand," the chemist told him with a straight face. "It's not us. This company only wants innovation that has stood the test of time."

Once Rob understood that the organization was primed to be excessively cautious, he knew that in order to foster innovation, he would have to do more than get the chemists excited about what they could create and facilitate their collaboration. He would have to help the organization as a whole reset itself to prevent excessive caution.

As Rob subsequently explained to the chemists— and then to the company's leadership team— inoculating any group of people against Sabotage by Excessive Caution takes at least two steps.

The first is developing the ability to understand people's "default" tendencies (including your own) and what sort of impact they have (and have had) on their working group.

Shari Steinman, a psychologist at the University of Virginia, points out that "a lot of individuals with anxiety interpret ambiguous information in a negative way."[2] So if your boss or the leader of your group is anxious and likely to respond in negative or pessimistic ways—and thus likely to advocate for caution at every turn—anticipate his or her reactions. Be ready to press (diplomatically) for the facts that led to his or her concerns and to use the "Yes, and" technique. If you are in charge, make sure that whoever is making decisions doesn't have a tendency to be overly cautious.

What if you're in charge and your natural tendency is to worry and be cautious in most situations? If you're the potential Excessive Caution Saboteur, and you know it, then build in the checks and balances you need to be sure you aren't holding your group back. Identify someone who is more action-oriented and not overly cautious. And when you find yourself drawing back from taking action, or when you have a "Yes, but" response on your lips, call a time-out and turn to that trusted advisor. Bounce your ideas off of them—not to identify a solution, but to ensure that your response, to his or her mind, isn't too hesitant or negative.

The second step to inoculating against Sabotage by Excessive Caution is learning how to see, with objectivity, the effect that your behavior, or the behaviors of others, is having on the group as a whole and changing the behaviors that promote the sabotage. Think about teaching kids to swim. Say they fall into the water by accident. You scream, jump in after them with your arms flailing, pull them out by any body- or bathing-suit-part you can get a hand on, swaddle them in a towel, and rush them into the locker room clutching them tightly. They're not going to develop confidence around the water. If, on the other hand, you jump in, lift them up but not out, laugh, and say, "Not so fast, dude! Here, let's jump in together and I'll show you how much fun it is to float," they're likely to have a healthier attitude toward water.

Doing this in an organization or group setting means training people to focus on the positive aspects of issues and opportunities, rather than on the potential negatives. It means watching your language and your behavior and countering the negative language of others. It means learning how to emphasize the positive possibilities rather than the negative when you're setting expectations, and making that kind of emphasis a habit. Say, "Do this," instead of "Don't do that." Or ask, "What's the weather today?" instead of "Is it going to rain?" Focus on what you expect people to do ("Use your great passing skills, and score a lot of baskets!"), not on what you expect them not to do ("Remember not to commit any fouls!"). Focus less on what people can do wrong, and more on what they can do right. Help others do it, too. Take a lesson from the popular saying, "Things are rarely as good, or as bad, as they seem."

Another step you can take in order to inoculate your organization against Sabotage by Excessive Caution is to plan for "What if" scenarios. This step can be expensive, but if you do it regularly, you will ease the sort of insecurity that can lead to sabotage. It involves taking the time to talk through what you, or your group, would do if a worst-case scenario came to be. Don't dwell on this step (remember, you want to emphasize the positive), but if you say, "Well, here's what we would do if . . ." then people might feel a little more prepared. In the process, you might even identify a few tools to help you prevent that worst-case scenario. Take the Bear Worrier: In a discussion about worst-case scenarios—running into a bear— you might talk through escape plans, and do a little research into how to deal with bears if you encounter one in the woods of New England. In the process, you could also discuss how to prevent running into a bear in the first place—such as storing food suspended from a tree far away from campers.

Have you used up some valuable time doing this? Yes. But it may be time well spent if it results in peace of mind. It's like buying insurance: You get peace of mind in advance, but it's not free.

The Most Personal
Tactic

Sabotage by Excessive Caution may be the most personal of all of the tactics in this book, feeding as it often does on the anxieties that people have. It also may be the most overt form of sabotage in the book; that is, many of the forms of sabotage articulated by the OSS result in delay, but "avoiding haste" is essentially the same thing as saying "slow down" outright. Preventing this kind of sabotage is complex; it requires attack from multiple fronts; and it's just plain hard to keep up the battle consistently over time. As Brent Walder told us: "Keep in mind that it's easier to follow cautious advice. Being overly cautious requires less of a person than moving ahead."

The good news is that in a group setting, when balanced views prevail repeatedly, eventually a culture that is highly resistant to Sabotage by Excessive Caution develops. You might even build a place where innovation can withstand the test of time.

8

Sabotage by Is-It-Really-Our-Call?

Be worried about the propriety of any
decision—raise the question of whether
such action as is contemplated lies
within the jurisdiction of the group
or whether it might conflict with
the policy of some higher echelon.

D ecisions are the livelihood of organizations. An organization's accomplishments and setbacks, its ability or inability to seize an opportunity, are the direct result of a decision someone made—or a decision someone failed to make. Yet despite their importance, decisions frequently stall and take longer than they should, ultimately keeping an organization from reaching its full potential.

There's no faster way to stall decision-making than by seeding doubt in the minds of those who are making the decisions: Do they have the right to make the call at all? Are they overstepping their boundaries? Will they get in trouble?

The OSS understood this—and knew that creating a low-grade level of anxiety in the staff of enemy institutions already stressed by war conditions would have a great impact on the ability of those institutions to make effective decisions. That's why this last sabotage tactic in the *Simple Sabotage Field Manual* encouraged allies to cast doubt on every decision being made by calling into question the jurisdiction of those who were trying to make it. They wanted to attack their enemy where it would hurt them the most: in their decision-making processes.

The inadvertent Is-It-Really-Our-Call Saboteurs lurking in your group have no such intentions— they don't *want* to undermine your group's abilities to make effective decisions. But they can't help themselves. Whenever people stall a decision or cast doubt in the minds of their co-workers with statements like, "Is making this decision even within our purview?" or "Shouldn't we check in with others in case we step on the toes of someone else (especially our boss)?" they are posing a significant threat to your organization's livelihood. A threat you probably haven't noticed.

As with the other acts of sabotage described in this book, cautioning co-workers to seriously consider whether a decision they are about to make is "really our call" is perfectly good behavior. If the roles of everyone involved in a decision are well defined and it appears that someone is overstepping his or her boundaries (whether on purpose or not), it is the right thing to speak up.

But when the reason for questioning the right of a group to make a decision stems from either a lack of confidence or systemic ambiguity—ambiguity about what is being decided and who is accountable for that decision—it crosses the line into sabotage. In these cases, the inadvertent Is-It-Really-Our-Call Saboteur is fanning the flames of weakness in the group's processes, rather than overcoming it. Individuals who commit Sabotage by Is-It-Really-Our-Call perpetuate conflicts over who has the final say because the path to the final say isn't clear to them.

The key to stopping and preventing this kind of sabotage is to understand its roots. Here we offer the four most common causes of this insidious sabotage—and how to counter them.

Lack of Confidence

Often, the reason why people question the authority of a group to make a decision stems from lack of confidence—in themselves or in the group. Unsure of whether they are capable of making the decision, these saboteurs try to halt the decision-making process—and negatively affect the productivity of the organization—by questioning the group's jurisdiction.

The source of this lack of confidence varies but often falls into one of three broad categories:

- The saboteur has a tendency to be overly cautious. This person worries unnecessarily about the possible "worst-case scenarios" of a decision and, not wanting to be held responsible if the decision turns out to have negative consequences, questions the advisability of proceeding without a green light from the higher-ups. (See Chapter 7 for more on how fear is often the root motivation of these Excessive Caution Saboteurs.)

- The saboteur possesses little faith in his or her abilities—or those of the team. Such people may be timid, doubtful of their own expertise; they might not believe they have the knowledge necessary to make the decision in question. Or even if they are confident in their experience and ability, they don't feel that team members are up to par and should be trusted to influence the final decision. Maybe they are worried that authority has been misplaced and belongs with someone who has more of a handle on things.

- The saboteur has been reprimanded in the past for making a decision on his or her own instead of turning responsibility for it over to a higher-up—and that person is loath to find himself or herself in this position again. "Once burned, twice shy," as the saying goes. Such inadvertent saboteurs have been conditioned, in other words, to commit sabotage—to question whether they or the group has the right to make decisions independently.

When Is-It-Really-Our-Call Saboteurs unnecessarily question the right of the group to make a decision independently because they lack confidence, your best bet is to nip this action in the bud. Even if you are not in charge of the group, a little leadership can go a long way here. When someone in your group asks, "Is this really the group to make this decision?" stare that person down and say: "Damn right it is. We were asked to do such-and-such and that's just what we're doing. So let's plow ahead. We're on track to accomplish just what we set out to do, so let's not get sidetracked."

If you are in charge of the group or are the manager who delegated the decision to the group, you can prevent Sabotage by Is-It-Really-Our-Call in the future by exploring and addressing the source of the saboteur's lack of confidence.

If you find that you are dealing with an overly cautious person, we encourage you to turn back to Chapter 7 for some tips on how to respond. If you are dealing with someone who doesn't believe he or she has the ability or expertise to make decisions, you might need to work with that person one-on-one to boost his or her confidence and ability to make judgments and decisions independently.

If the person doesn't have faith in the other group members' expertise or experience, you'll want to examine the merits of those concerns. If there's truth to them, you might need to work to get your group's skills up to par. And if the concerns are unwarranted, you might need to spend time building trust within your team.

Finally, if the saboteur has been burned in the past and that experience now haunts him or her enough to lead to inadvertent Sabotage by Is-It-Really-Our-Call, then you need to understand what happened to this person before, acknowledge how difficult that experience must have been, and explain how the current situation is different.

An Ambiguous Definition of the Decision That Needs to Be Made

It's amazing how many times we've seen a team assembled and resources mobilized to make a decision on an issue without clear articulation of, and agreement on, the decision to be made. If you and your colleagues find yourselves sitting around the table quibbling over what the group is trying to decide, then watch out: It's easy, in this scenario, for the Is-It-Really-Our-Call Saboteur to question whether the group has the right to make the decision at all—especially since the group will have a hard time answering that question, given that the answer probably depends on how the decision is defined in the first place.

Consider the case of a high-end boat manufacturer that was falling farther behind its competitors in the market. Facing the task of deciding how to reduce the cost of its boats, a team of company executives from various functions instead fell into a series of long, contentious meetings. In particular, Bill from marketing and Lori from product development couldn't agree on which function should take the lead role. Each of them, unsure of their authority and worried about doing the wrong thing, kept trying to push the responsibility off on the other. Bill repeatedly offered a variation on this comment: "I don't think this call can rest with us. I think you need to get right with your budget, and then let us know what we have to work with. Everything you want to include costs an arm and a leg." Lori repeatedly countered with something along the lines of, "We can't make this call without you telling us what our standard features have to be. Given the shape this company is in, that's a marketing issue. You have the research—or at least you should."

The team didn't make any progress until it went to the company's president for help. Faced with a room full of angry people, the president finally realized that she needed to clarify the decisions to be made by breaking them into smaller pieces. First, she had the existing team hold a brainstorming session, with no decision on the table at all. At that session, she asked the team to exchange ideas about the types of boat features that seemed to be most desirable to customers, about the latest developments in features, and about various ways to save costs. No one was responsible for deciding anything in that meeting.

Then, in consultation with her CFO, the head of marketing, and the head of product development, the president set a target range for the cost per boat. After that, she asked the product development department to come up with a range of features that could lower the cost of the boats. Then, she tasked Bill, as head of marketing, with engaging the marketing people to decide on a set of features from the list with an eye toward what the customer wanted and what the competition currently offered. It was then up to the president to approve that decision.

The lesson here: Be sure to define explicitly each decision that needs to be made. Assess the decision on the table against the people you are thinking of bringing together to address it. You might then create a team charter—a formal description of the issue the team is considering and the decisions that the team is expected to make. If you do this, be sure to have the manager or person who called the team together sign off on the charter. Once the charter is created, remind the team of it frequently. If you are in charge of the group, you can do this by bringing it up every time your group meets. For example, a school Board of Trustees we know starts each monthly meeting with a clear purpose outlining what decisions need to be made at the meeting or are being explored by various committees, whose input will be necessary to make those decisions, and what process will be followed to make each decision.

If you aren't in charge of the group and suspect there's ambiguity about what the group needs to make a decision on, speak up. Try to seek clarity from the group itself or whoever assigned your group the task to make the decision in the first place.

Albert Einstein reportedly said that if he had one hour to save the world, he would spend fifty-five minutes defining the problem and only five minutes finding the solution. Take the time to make sure your group understands exactly what the decision is and frame it well.

No One Knows Who's In Charge

When a group is tasked with making a decision, if any ambiguity exists over who does what—who needs to provide input and be part of the deliberation, who is responsible for making the final call—the door is wide open for the Is-It-Really-Our-Call Saboteur to halt the decision-making process altogether.

Recall the inherent tensions among the various people trying to save the boat company. Missing from that group was a leader who could prioritize the issues. Until the team members sought out the company president, and the president reset the decision-making process, Lori and Bill had taken turns being unhappy with the direction the group was taking and thereby stymying progress. They might have done so indefinitely.

In Chapter 3, we explored how to use the RACI decision-making model to clarify the roles of members of committees or groups that have been formed to tackle a special project or decision. Another useful tool for doing this and determining who should be involved in the first place is the "decision rights framework."[1] This framework encourages you to assign individuals to one of the following "decision rights":

- **The right to provide input before a decision is made:** This right is allocated to those who must provide a critical input—data, analysis, or recommendation—into the decision-making process. (As it turned out for the boat company, the product group provided critical input to the marketing group, in the form of a menu of boat features, so the marketing group could decide what to include on the boats to bring the cost down.)

- **The right to make a decision in light of the input gathered.** This right is allocated to only one person to ensure clear accountability. (For the boat company, that decision fell to Bill, the head of marketing.)

- **The right to ratify or veto the decision.** Typically, this right is assigned to the manager who delegated the responsibility to make a decision (the boat company's president).

- **The right to be notified of the decision after the fact.** This right is allocated to those who will need to know what the final decision is because it affects their ability to do their work or to make other decisions. (The boat company's product development team would need to know what features had been selected as standard so they could work from there to develop option packages.)

Perhaps no two roles are more important to delineate and clarify in order to prevent Sabotage by Is-It-Really-Our-Call than that of the individual who is allocated the right to make a decision and that of the person who is allocated the right to ratify or veto that decision.

Managers are trained to allocate the right to make decisions to people who are in positions to make informed decisions and perhaps execute them as well. In other words, they are trained to delegate decisions. When a decision is delegated, responsibility for the decision is handed over, but managers stay in the information loop and reserve the right to intervene or make the final call—they reserve the right to ratify or veto the decision. They rarely abdicate responsibility for a decision; that is, they don't typically hand over ownership of the decision to a decision maker and then disappear from the process. Most decisions are delegated, not abdicated.

The problem is that often managers say or unwittingly imply that they are giving a group or someone total ownership of a decision—that they are abdicating the responsibility of the decision—when in fact they are handing the group responsibility for coming up with a well-formulated recommendation for a final decision that they will then ratify. In other words, they are delegating the responsibility for the decision.

Take this example. Louis, the head of eCommerce for a luxury retailer, tells one of his direct reports, Elisa, that the company needs a fulfillment strategy for their operations in China. "Please form a team and make a final decision on what we should do," Louis tells Elisa. But does Louis mean that Elisa's team is to make a *recommendation* on what decision the company ought to make, or to actually make the final call on the decision and execute it? No one bothers to ask or to clarify.

Elisa forms a team, and after weeks of gathering data and deliberating, the team is close to a decision. But then Dianne, one of the members of the decision team—and someone who is unhappy with the strategy option that is emerging as the group's favorite— sends Louis an email complaining about what the group is about to decide and presents him with an alternative option. Louis agrees with Dianne, so he instructs Elisa and her team to pursue this new option and implement it.

Louis became what Ken Blanchard calls a Seagull Manager in his book *Leadership and the One Minute*

Manager. He flew in, made a lot of noise, dumped on everybody, and then flew out. Elisa's team members, who worked for weeks, feel alienated and are left to wonder why Louis gave them ownership of a decision if he was planning to make the final decision himself anyway. The reality is that Louis never handed them complete ownership of the decision, but rather delegated responsibility for a well-formulated recommendation that he needed to be comfortable executing. He always intended to have the final say on the decision, and as soon as he was comfortable with a decision (in this case Dianne's), he made it.

When managers fail to communicate exactly the decision rights that they are allocating, the door is opened for the Is-It-Really-Our-Call Saboteurs, like Dianne, to question (even implicitly, as she did by going behind Elisa's back) whether the group has jurisdiction over a decision.

If a manager asks you to "make a decision," take the time to clarify exactly what he or she means. Is your manager asking for a recommendation? Or is he or she really handing you the right both to make the decision and to ratify it? Either way, ask your manager how he or she would like to be involved in the process so you have a clear understanding of the input and guidance that your manager would like to provide during the process, if any at all.

Regardless of what framework you use to clearly

define the roles of everyone involved in the decision-making process, be sure to remind the players of their roles often. One client of ours makes a habit of asking each person, at the beginning of a decision-making meeting, what role he or she is playing in the process. The more these decision roles are visible and entrenched, the lower the risk that Is-It-Really-Our-Call Saboteurs will question jurisdiction—and if they do, the answers should be apparent.

Managers Who Are Too Quick to Override a Group's Decision

In an ideal situation, once managers have delegated a decision and defined the roles of everyone involved in it, they will stay in the loop but not interfere with the decision-making *process*. They will advise the group as needed but wait for the group to deliver a decision that they can then ratify or veto.

In practice, this is not always the case. Too often, managers intervene in the decision-making process at the mere appearance of conflict. And Is-It-Really-Our-Call Saboteurs are quick to seize on this managerial weakness. When frustrated with the decision-making process, or disappointed in the

direction in which the group is headed, these saboteurs implicitly question the group's right to make
the final decision by going behind the group's back,
as Dianne did, and voice concerns directly to the
manager. Overreacting to the saboteur's concerns,
the manager gets involved in the decision process,
confusing and derailing the work of the group making the decision.

There's no more insidious a form of sabotaging
a decision than when an individual goes around or
above the current decision maker—like a child who
appeals to Dad after Mom says "no." When managers get involved at the request of a disgruntled team
member, their involvement often undermines the
current decision-making process and the people who
were delegated the responsibility to carry it out.

The members of the group feel alienated and de-
feated. What's the point of carefully considering and
arriving at a decision if the boss is going intervene
at the behest of a single dissenter in their group and
question or override it? They will think twice about
investing themselves too much when the manager
asks them to make another decision.

So if you've delegated a decision to a group and
are approached by a disgruntled Is-It-Really-Our-
Call Saboteur who is attempting to do an end run
around the rest of the group by coming directly to
you with his or her complaints, ask a lot of questions,
but don't necessarily jump into the fray. Listen to the

saboteur's concerns and then decide whether they truly warrant your intervention.

To decide whether to step in or not, keep in mind that not all decisions carry the same weight. Our experience suggests that most of an organization's success hinges on about 20 percent of the decisions the company makes. You should focus your energy on this critical 20 percent. Putting these critical decisions into two categories can help you concentrate your efforts and involvement on the decisions that are most important. Without some degree of prioritization you run the risk that all decisions will be treated the same, which means important ones won't be treated with the care they deserve.

The first category includes the decisions that entail the most value. Most of these relate to strategy and are typically one-off decisions. For instance, a school district decides whether to acquire an available piece of real estate to open a middle school. A consulting firm decides to move into a new service line. These big decisions lead to big payoffs, if you get them right.

The second category of decisions comprises those decisions that are more routine. They are made frequently, and if done well, can significantly affect your results. For instance, consulting firms make regular decisions on how to deploy staff across client engagements. The editor-in-chief of a magazine decides which articles to include. These types of decisions are made every day across the organization. Some of the decisions in this category may be just as important to your success.

By delineating which decisions deserve your direct attention and involvement, you'll be able to better assess when and how to respond when you are approached with concerns about a decision you've delegated.

Go Forward and Decide

Successful organizations make and execute decisions faster than their competitors. But so often, when ambiguity persists inside organizations about the decisions to be made or about who is responsible for making them, the door is opened wide for Is-It-Really-Our-Call Saboteurs to walk right through and cast a shadow of doubt on the people involved in making those decisions. The effect can be devastating, as making decisions takes longer than it should, opportunities are missed, and people involved become alienated and resentful, ultimately driving an organization into mediocrity—just what the OSS intended when it included this final tactic in the *Simple Sabotage Field Manual*.

Our message is that, regardless of the size of an organization, every leader—whether he or she is in charge of a group or is part of a team responsible for making a decision—can thwart Sabotage by Is-It-

Really-Our-Call by making sure the decision to be made is clearly defined and ensuring that who plays what roles during the decision-making process is understood and frequently communicated. With these two things in place, any would-be saboteur who questions the jurisdiction of the group can be turned away with the utmost confidence that not only is this the right group to make the decision, but the group will not be slowed down or derailed in making the decision with appropriate authority and speed.

9

Modern Sabotage by CC: Everyone

CC: Everyone. Send updates as
frequently as possible, including
in the distribution list anyone
even peripherally involved.

he OSS rules are timeless, but new technologies and organizational forms allow the development of new forms of sabotage all the time. If the OSS sabotage experts had been writing their manual today, we feel certain they would have added at least one additional sabotage technique involving email.

The research organization Radicati Group reports that the average corporate email user sends and receives about 121 emails a day.[1] Of course, many of us, and certainly people in executive positions, get far more than that. All of us now live under a ceaseless tide of inbound emails—far too many to fully process during an already busy day. We discard many without reading them, or after giving a cursory glance to the subject line or the first few sentences. And when the email consists of a string of emails stacked on top of the others, it's by no means a safe assumption that anyone will have read the full email trail or followed its content.

Why has there been such a proliferation of e-mails? How has this relatively new invention invaded our lives to the extent that, according to the consulting firm McKinsey and Company, 28 percent of the average workweek for managers and professionals is now dedicated to reading and answering email?[2]

Pure spam (advertisements) aside, the answer is simple: It's the evil "cc" option.

When the original *Simple Sabotage Field Manual* was written, a "cc" was just that—a carbon copy. A typist would insert two sheets of paper in the typewriter with a thin sheet of carbon paper—a waxy paper covered on one side with dry ink—between them. That way, a copy was made of whatever was typed. A strong typist might be able to make two copies, in which case one could be filed and the second passed along to someone other than the recipient. And so the convention came into being of putting "cc" on the bottom of the page to inform the recipient of who else would be seeing the document.

Photocopying was still in the future, so this was the only practical way to generate a second or third copy of a letter, memo, or report without going through the tedious process of retyping.

Today, of course, getting a copy of a document to multiple people at the same time is much simpler. When you compose an email, you simply tag on as many individuals or groups as you choose. Adding recipients is as easy as clicking on a button. You can hit "reply all" to effortlessly spray information in many directions at once. Much of the time, you cc or bcc an entire group or team distribution list to "inform them," "update them," or "keep them in the loop." But cc'ing one and all on an email isn't necessarily informing anyone. And the more people on the distribution list, the less likely that any individual recipient opens or reads or processes and understands its contents.

When people copy a large group of people or hit "reply all," in reality, they are giving themselves cover. Once they hit "send," nobody can come back and say "you never told me" or "you should have asked me" or "why didn't you keep me informed?" That person was copied, so that person knew—or should have known. That person was "told," although a word was never spoken.

The burden or responsibility of communication has been shifted. Now, the sender is off the hook, and everyone copied on an email is collectively implicated in the responsibility for whatever decisions, actions, or information lie, unread, in the clutter of a busy email inbox or at the bottom of a long email trail.

It's a saboteur's dream—one that wasn't available in 1944, but that certainly would have been included on the list of OSS sabotage tactics if it had been. In fact, Sabotage by CC: Everyone is a mainstay of modern work life. Inadvertent saboteurs in working groups of every size "cc" and "bcc" to their hearts' content, clogging people's email inboxes and slowing decision-making processes. And perhaps even more dangerous, they go about their business confident in the assumption that their colleagues or bosses are "informed" and will speak up if they aren't onboard with whatever they're doing.

With the amount of email that people receive these days, this is not an assumption that can be made.

It's relatively easy to see whether Sabotage by CC: Everyone is at work in your group. Take a good look at your own email inbox. How many messages are directed to you personally, and how many are there because you're on a distribution list? Are those emails relevant, or are they the ones that you quickly delete or stash in an electronic folder? Do the distribution lists seem overly broad? Is it clear why all the people on the list need to be kept in the loop on the topic of each email?

Most importantly, ask yourself whether people frequently assume that you've been informed of things simply because you were copied on an email. Do you find your peers and subordinates using phrases like "but I told you about that last week" when in fact the "telling" consisted of your being cc'd (along with many others) on an email?

If the answer is "yes," then you have some work to do.

Fixing Sabotage by CC: Everyone in the Moment

First, you need to learn how to stop this kind of sabotage as it is happening. After you realize that you have been sabotaged in this manner, you could cave in to a knee-jerk desire (which we have witnessed and which predictably ended badly) to respond in kind and fire back a nasty response to the entire organization or group, putting only one name on the

"To:" line and cc'ing everyone else. But that would be rude; we can assure you that this will only escalate the problem.

Instead, yours ought to be the measured, effective response. We recommend the following three steps.

Take Yourself Off as Many Distribution Lists as Possible

If your email inbox is cluttered with hundreds, or perhaps thousands, of unread messages that are routinely sent to a large group of people, take some time to evaluate how important and helpful these emails are to you. Does every one of them contain information that is critical for you to do your job? Or do they report data that you need occasionally or that you can look up at your convenience through a different mechanism? Or are they simply not necessary at all?

For example, you *need* to know things that pertain to your weekly schedule, or things that pertain to upcoming events or deadlines. But the content of many other emails you receive might simply be *nice* to know. The monthly update on the book club, for instance. The newsletter you thought would be interesting to receive but have never read. And then there's spam—content you don't need at all.

Your email system may already sort some of this

email for you, but you can probably hone this system even more. If some regular emails are not important to you, either filter them out or ask the sender to take you off the distribution list. If, on the other hand, the content has meaning to you but it's obvious that email isn't working as a means to get the information to you, then you need to . . .

Ask To Be Informed Personally When You Need to Know Something

Tell people (never your boss) that including you on a group email list as a cc recipient is not necessarily the same as informing you personally. If someone wants you to "know" something, he or she should contact you through a direct person-to-person communication—a meeting, a call, a text message, or a personal email. Let that person know that including you as a "cc" on a distribution list isn't an adequate substitute. In some cases, even a direct personal email isn't enough, unless it's clearly marked for your attention.

Let people know that if they haven't heard back from you in, say, forty-eight hours, they should send you a nudge. (If there's a deadline, then sooner, of course.) And remember: Any response on your part, even a simple "received," will indicate that you have read, or intend to read, the message.

Make Sure Subject Lines Include a Priority or Action Step

Any time you send an email that requires a response, let the recipient know in the first words of the subject line: RESPONSE REQUIRED. If it's time sensitive, then say TIME SENSITIVE or RESPONSE REQUIRED with the date included. And ask the people you deal with frequently to do the same; they should let you know when something requires your immediate attention.

While we're on the subject of subject lines, it's also a good idea to ask people to update the subject line when they are changing the topic of conversation. You should also do this yourself. It's easy to skip over the fifteenth back-and-forth email with a subject line of "Re: holiday party"—but what if that fifteenth reply was actually the beginning of a new conversation that should have been titled "Important Budget Question: Response Required"? The inadvertent saboteur treats an email conversation with someone as if it were an in-person conversation, where you can start on one topic and move to another without saying, "Now I'm going to change the subject." But an email conversation requires just that sort of blatant signaling. If you're going to change topics, begin a new email trail with a new subject line, or at least change the subject line of the email trail you're on.

Ending Sabotage
by CC: Everyone

Fortunately for us all, Sabotage by CC: Everyone can be conquered by taking the following steps.

Institute Regular Formal Updates

In one of his prior roles, Bob was indirectly responsible for twenty to thirty ongoing projects at any given time. If he had been copied on each email, or even a subset of the daily flow among the project managers, their teams, and the client executives, he would have drowned under a daily tsunami of inbound information. Fortunately, his firm had instituted a system of weekly "Flash Reports." On a single page, the project manager would inform all the relevant parties of the significant events of the past week and coming week, any outstanding significant issues, and scheduled meetings and calls. Rather than dig through thousands of emails, Bob (and others) could quickly and efficiently be brought up to speed on all the projects and then dig into detail as needed.

It's true that a structured update might take the form of an email with a distribution list, which we've suggested avoiding. The difference, though, is that this is a requested, anticipated update; it takes the place of thousands of extraneous communications; and the receivers are not on a "cc" list—they are the primary recipients.

A structured update might also take the form of a weekly call or video conference—whatever works best for your group and situation.

Make Sure That People Get the Information They Need

One of the factors driving email overload is a failure to tailor information to a specific audience. It's easy to send everything to everyone; but it takes effort to structure information for those who need to be informed differently from the way you structure information for those who are responsible for a decision, its implementation, and its outcome. It's not a good idea to include those who just need to be informed on every email correspondence intended for those who must take action, and (by contrast) including detailed implementation information in an email to everyone when the only people who need it are those who are taking action. Don't assume that people can separate the wheat from the chaff and determine what they should be reading.

Insist, too, that those who need to be informed on a matter have the information processed and presented in a way that is convenient for them, rather than ask them to pick and choose among a mass of unorganized data. As we said in Chapter 2, data isn't the same as useable insight. Being deluged with information is not the same as being informed. The sender has the obligation to do the "heavy lifting" to make sure the recipient is truly informed.

Create a Culture That Knows Email Is Not a Substitute for Personal Dialogue

We've all seen those families eating at restaurants where everyone at the table is staring at the screen of their own personal device. Smartphones and tablets seem to be displacing talking to another person as the primary way of communicating.

This may be convenient (and, unfortunately, the way the world seems to be headed), but we wonder whether the information being exchanged is particularly important or time sensitive. If the quality of the information being exchanged is important, or if you are going back and forth on an issue with someone or a group, maybe it's time to put the screen away. Consider asking to continue the dialogue in person. A brief meeting or a phone call, although more time-consuming than a text or email, can often result in a much clearer understanding among all parties concerned. In the words of St. Augustine, *Solvitur ambulando* (It is solved by walking)—in this case, just walk down the hall.

We are confident that you will be able to defeat Sabotage by CC: Everyone in your group or organization. In fact, we're confident that you'll be able to defeat and/or defend against all of the types of inadvertent sabotage we've covered in this book. But we'll leave you with this thought: Where there are people working together, and where new organizational forms emerge and technology advances, there will always be accidental, unwitting sabotage. Be vigilant!

Acknowledgments

We owe special thanks to Regina Maruca, our thought partner and editor, who helped steer this work from the germ of an idea to a complete manuscript; to Katherine Flynn, our superagent at Kneerim & Williams; to the insightful, multitalented Genoveva Llosa, senior editor at HarperOne, and her colleagues there, including Hannah Rivera, Kim Dayman, Melinda Mullin, and Lisa Zuniga, each of whom had the vision and the imagination to understand what *Simple Sabotage* could be and how best to convey its messages in published form; to Lucia Gumbs of the Strategic Offsites Group, who kept us on track and on target; to the rest of the team from the Strategic Offsites Group, all of whom played key roles: Bobby Asadishad, Michael Katzman, Andrew McIlwraith, Dan Prager, and Sarah Weiskittel. We are most grateful to them and to all of the people who agreed to be interviewed, quoted, and further pressed into intellectual service in the course of our work.

Notes

Introduction

1. Prepared under the direction of William J. Donovan, director of Strategic Services, *Simple Sabotage Field Manual, Strategic Services Field Manual No. 3* (Office of Strategic Services, January 17, 1944), 28.

Chapter 1: Sabotage by Obedience

1. This story is told in James T. Ziegenfuss Jr., *Customer Friendly: The Organizational Architecture of Service* (University Press of America, 2007), 135.

Chapter 2: Sabotage by Speech

1. See http://www.urbandictionary.com/define. php?term=Long+Talker.

Chapter 3: Sabotage by Committee

1. Alan Deutschman, "Inside the Mind of Jeff Bezos," *Fast Company,* August 2004,

http://www.fastcompany.com/50541/
inside-mind-jeff-bezos.

2. Joan S. Lublin, "Smaller Boards Get
Bigger Returns," *Wall Street Journal,* August
26, 2014, http://www.wsj.com/articles/
smaller-boards-get-bigger-returns-1409078628.

Chapter 4: Sabotage by Irrelevant Issues

1. Robert M. Galford and Anne Seibold Drapeau,
*The Trusted Leader: Bringing Out the Best in Your
People and Your Company* (Atria, 2011), 67.

Chapter 6: Sabotage by Reopening Decisions

1. Noel Tichy and David Ulrich, "The Leadership
Challenge—A Call for the Transformational
Leader." *Sloan Management Review* 26, no. 1
(1984): 63.

Chapter 7: Sabotage by Excessive Caution

1. Tina Fey, *BossyPants* (Regan Arthur, 2011).

2. Amy Nordrum, "Hacking Fear," *Psychology
Today,* September 2, 2014, https://www.psychology
today.com/articles/201410/hacking-fear.

Chapter 8: Sabotage by Is-It-Really-Our-Call?

1. Decision Rights Framework: Credit, Rob
Galford.

Chapter 9: Sabotage by CC: Everyone

1. "Email Statistics Report, 2014 – 2018," The Radicati Group, Inc., Editor: Sara Radicati, PhD, http://www.radicati.com/wp/wp-content/uploads/2014/01/Email-Statistics-Report-2014-2018-Executive-Summary.pdf.

2. Michael Chui, James Manyika, Jacques Bughin, Richard Dobbs, Charles Roxburgh, Hugo Sarrazin, Geoffrey Sands, and Magdalena Westergren, "The social economy: Unlocking value and productivity through social technologies," McKinsey Global Institute Report, McKinsey &Company, July 2012; http://www.mckinsey.com/insights/high_tech_telecoms_internet/the_social_economy.

About the Authors

Robert M. Galford, Managing Partner of the Center for Leading Organizations, divides his time between teaching Executive Education programs and working with senior executives at the world's leading public, private, and governmental entities. Rob is a Leadership Fellow in Executive Education at the Harvard Graduate School of Design and is on the teaching faculty of the National Association of Corporate Directors. He is a member of the Board of Directors of Forrester Research. Rob is the coauthor of *The Trusted Advisor, The Trusted Leader, Your Leadership Legacy,* and numerous articles published in the *Harvard Business Review* and other major publications.

Bob Frisch, Managing Partner of the Strategic Offsites Group, is considered one of the world's leading strategic facilitators, having designed and conducted offsites in fifteen countries with companies ranging from Fortune 10 multinationals to German *Mittelstand* family businesses. Bob is the author of four major *Harvard Business Review* articles, including the classic "Off-Sites That Work." Another of Bob's articles, "When Teams Can't Decide," was named one of the *Harvard Business Review*'s ten "must read" articles on teams. Bob's best-selling first book, *Who's in the Room? How Great Leaders Structure and Manage the Teams Around Them,* is distributed in twelve countries.

Cary Greene, Partner of the Strategic Offsites Group, consults with boards and senior executives on large-scale transformations, challenging strategic issues, and leadership conferences. Earlier in his career, he cofounded a strategy and technology consulting firm, which twice landed on the Inc. 500 list as one of the fastest-growing private companies. Cary has been a guest lecturer at a leading business school, and his latest article, "Leadership Summits That Work" (coauthored with Bob Frisch), was published in the *Harvard Business Review*.